COOPERATIVE LEARNING
Critical Thinking and Collaboration
Across the Curriculum

COOPERATIVE LEARNING
Critical Thinking and Collaboration
Across the Curriculum

DENNIS M. ADAMS
University of Minnesota
Duluth

MARY E. HAMM
San Francisco State
University

C H A R L E S   C   T H O M A S   •   P U B L I S H E R
Springfield • Illinois • U.S.A.

WITHDRAWN
NORTHEASTERN ILLINOIS
UNIVERSITY LIBRARY

Published and Distributed Throughout the World by

CHARLES C THOMAS • PUBLISHER
2600 South First Street
Springfield, Illinois 62794-9265

© *1990 by* CHARLES C THOMAS • PUBLISHER

ISBN 0-398-05644-7

Library of Congress Catalog Card Number: 89-27601

With **THOMAS BOOKS** *careful attention is given to all details of manufacturing
and design. It is the Publisher's desire to present books that are satisfactory as to their
physical qualities and artistic possibilities and appropriate for their particular use.*
THOMAS BOOKS *will be true to those laws of quality that assure a good name
and good will.*

Printed in the United States of America
SC-R-3

Library of Congress Cataloging-in-Publication Data

Adams, Dennis M.
    Cooperative learning : critical thinking and collaboration across
the curriculum / Dennis M. Adams, Mary E. Hamm.
      p. cm.
    Includes bibliographical references.
    ISBN 0-398-05644-7
    1. Team learning approach in education. 2. Group work in
education. 3. Critical thinking. I. Hamm, Mary. II. Title.
LB1032.A33 1990
371.3'95—dc20   89-27601
                                            CIP

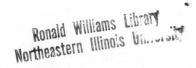

PREFACE

Schools have traditionally structured learning in an individualistic and competitive manner. Numerous research studies and educational reports have pointed out that these solitary models tend to make students overly passive and indifferent to what is being taught. This book considers a wide range of more active collaborative possibilities for restructuring classrooms, reinvigorating the basic curriculum, and using technology to foster group interdependence and achievement. Attention is also given to helping teachers structure cooperative groups so that they can teach thinking skills across the curriculum.

Interest in collaborative models is growing rapidly as reliable research evidence increasingly points to cooperative learning as a promising practice for improving instruction. Even the *Associated Press* contributed to the trend by sending out a story to newspapers around the country that referred to cooperative learning as "the wave of the future" in education. The biggest argument over its use seems to be coming from proponents who favor different methods of implementation.

Using collaborative learning activities means structuring student interaction in small mixed-ability groups, encouraging mutual interdependence, and providing for individual accountability. In this atmosphere of mutual helpfulness students are supposed to talk to one another as they try to resolve issues through face-to-face discussion. These kind of cooperative learning arrangements encourage pupils to learn by assimilating their ideas and creating new knowledge through interaction with others. The teacher organizes the classroom, teaches social skills, encourages critical thinking, and responds to emerging insights.

This book is intended as a practical guide to issues, ideas, trends, and instructional methods for structuring collaborative work in basic skill areas. Establishing the conditions for cooperative learning and higher level thinking—as well as providing activities that can serve as examples—

is the focus of the volume. The intent is to help teachers get started with (and sustain) learning "teams" where students work together in a way that allows everybody to contribute to reaching common goals.

D. M. A.
M. E. H.

ACKNOWLEDGMENTS

Linda Miller-Cleary generously contributed her case study, "The Presence of Peers," to Chapter 4.

We would also like to acknowledge the important contribution of Vern Simula and Aliceon Stillman to the mainstreaming chapter. A special note of thanks to Mary Ann Rotondi for allowing us to try out many of the activities in her classroom.

CONTENTS

COOPERATIVE LEARNING
Critical Thinking and Collaboration
Across the Curriculum

1

COOPERATIVE LEARNING
AND TODAY'S STUDENTS:
KNOWLEDGE BUILDING FOR
TOMORROW'S WORKPLACE

A major theme of the flood of educational reports released in the 1980s calls for recapturing our national vision of a highly educated citizenry. Those with a more practical bent also point to the need for a skilled and motivated workforce to sustain us into the next decade and beyond. The various suggestions all involve a fundamental change in educational perspective.[1] One of the most significant suggestions is that democratically planned cooperative work and educational experiences can make a difference.

Many of these reports strike at the heart of guiding educational customs and organizational structures. Some place democratically constructed collaborative efforts at the center of learning and teaching. A suggestion of the university-based Holmes Group, as well as the Carnegie Corporation Council on Education, is to break large schools into smaller units and organize teachers and students into reasonably sized democratic communities of learners. In these cooperative learning environments students would be taught by teachers who would be free to plan how their group would make the best use of time, without bells breaking up group projects.

Cooperative learning is a good example of how schools can build on the tendency of students who enjoy actively working together in groups. By tapping this natural energy, seen everyday on the playground, teachers can enhance students' learning and thinking skills by designing their lessons around mixed-ability teamwork. Whether it's conceptual development, problem solving, or critical thinking, a collaborative approach has

---

1. Education Commission of the States: *One Third of a Nation: A Report of the Commission on Minority Participation in Education and American Life.* Washington, D.C., American Council on Education, 1988.

shown that it has the potential for developing these concepts while improving self-esteem.[2]

Today's Students and Their Future in the Workforce

Schools today have diverse student populations. One out of three children live in poverty according to a 1988 study by The Carnegie Foundation for the Advancement of Teaching. Alienation, poor health care programs, drug abuse, nutrition-related deficiencies and low self-esteem are common problems. Many of these students miss out on educational advantages from early childhood education to job training. Even students who come from homes that place a high value on education will have trouble living up to those values if there are constraints and limited opportunities in their community.

Many pupils today are bored in school. Many drop out. For students who stay in, schools frequently offer little encouragement to those who have talents extending beyond the ability to manipulate words and numbers. Some youngsters in inner-city classrooms have the tough-mindedness ("street smarts") that could assist them in becoming successful leaders and workers. They have learned how to beat the odds and fight the daily battles of personal survival. Many of these students value team sports and the cooperation needed to succeed. What they lack are the academic skills and world knowledge to "make it" in the literacy-intensive workplace. They are frequently caught between deteriorating schools and a precipitous drop in job possibilities.

It's important that teachers and the curricula be sensitive to the culture and interests of students. If these needs are not met many students will escape from the negative consequences of "poor academic performance" and seek satisfaction outside of school.

Schools frequently relegate disadvantaged students to lower tracks where they have the *least* access to the best teachers and an enriched curriculum. The mission of an educational system in a democracy goes beyond "the basics" to helping all of our students develop intellectual talents, civic understanding, a comprehension of humanistic/scientific traditions and the ability to think critically. Grouping decisions often become self-fulfilling prophecies, with few minorities in college-bound programs. For the advantaged student, in top ability groups, the empha-

---

2. Slavin, R.: *Cooperative Learning: Student Teams.* Washington, D.C., National Education Association, 1987.

sis is on critical thinking, creativity, and problem solving; for those at the bottom it's more often basic skills, conformity, and discipline.[3] Cooperative learning with mixed-ability teams offers one alternative to changing the tracking equation.

Schools are not alone in their attempts to meet the needs of a diverse clientele. American companies are finding they have to restructure the way they organize people and tasks as they try to meet growing international competition. The world of work is finding a shortage of highly skilled individuals who know how to work in groups, analyze what's going on, figure out how to do it better, make decisions, and be more than cogs in a machine. Many of today's workers simply don't have the skills they need to contribute effectively to the process. The industry-based Committee for Economic Development recently committed the private sector to strategies for combating the rapid decay of American education. Even the chief executive officers from some of the Fortune 500 companies came to the conclusion that *"investing in children—particularly the children of poverty—is the best investment we can make.... We all must share in the promise of America. America cannot prosper in the next century without greater investment in our schools and close attention to helping all students learn."*

One of IBM's top scientists, John Armstrong, suggests that the country is living on borrowed time. He points out that despite all the discussions about technological competitiveness, if the lack of scientific interest and low levels of achievement for children continue, it will leave us behind the rest of the world.[4]

By 1992 the United States is expected to experience the greatest shortage of skilled labor in its history. At the very time we are facing a labor shortage, we have a poverty surplus. This is a problem that is at least as much political as it is educational. David Kearns, chairman of the Xerox Corporation, points out that lack of leadership and poor performance by the American educational system is placing the United States at a terrible competitive disadvantage when it comes to producing innovative strategies. He suggests that we look to the smartest high-tech companies for models as national leadership rallies support for direct public action on educational issues. "How dare we consign our kids to two different

---

3. Hochschild, J.: *The New American Dilemma: Liberal Democracy and School Desegration.* New Haven, Yale University Press, 1984.

4. Armstrong, J. Paper presented at 1989 IBM Conference. New York.

futures."[5] The point here is that a broad range of fiscally conservative corporate figures are very concerned with the fact that the bulk of the labor pool in the nineties will be both disadvantaged and poorly educated. And they are becoming strong supporters of educational reform.

Opening Educational Opportunity Structures

*The ultimate test of a moral society is the
kind of world it leaves to its children.*
— Dietrich Bonhoeffer

Learning involves more than educators and students. Everyone is involved, either directly in the education of children or indirectly in structuring the world in which they live. If educators are to contribute to a solution to the problem of untapped human resources, educators will have to recognize the complex psychological, social, and institutional conditions that give rise to today's schooling difficulties. Cutting through the murky sludge of educational and social inertia requires focusing on overall sociopolitical structures as well as the specific characteristics of effective instruction.

Teachers have enormous power over how students view themselves. That power can be used to develop talent and release energy . . . or it can cause a crippling sense of inadequacy and failure. Unless the organization of the school and classroom environment provide for positive interaction between the whole spectrum of students, invalid stereotypes and preconceptions will be reinforced. If children from all races and backgrounds don't work together on an equal footing in school, then nothing is going to change the fact that they are valued differently and are not considered capable of working together for common goals.[6] For today's population of students, academic knowledge must also connect multi-cultural studies with self-sufficiency and the critical thinking skills necessary for dealing with an environment where change is the one constraint.

One of the most useful educational ideas recently advanced for enhancing learning and connecting schooling to the world of work is collaborative learning.[7] In this teacher-organized interactive learning environment

---

5. Kearns, D.: *Winning the Brain Race: A Bold Plan To Make Our Schools Competitive*, Institute for Contemporary Studies, 1987.

6. Edelman, M.: *Families in Peril: An Agenda for Social Change.* Cambridge, MA., Harvard University Press, 1989.

7. Holmes Group: *Forum.* 3 (1), Fall, 1988.

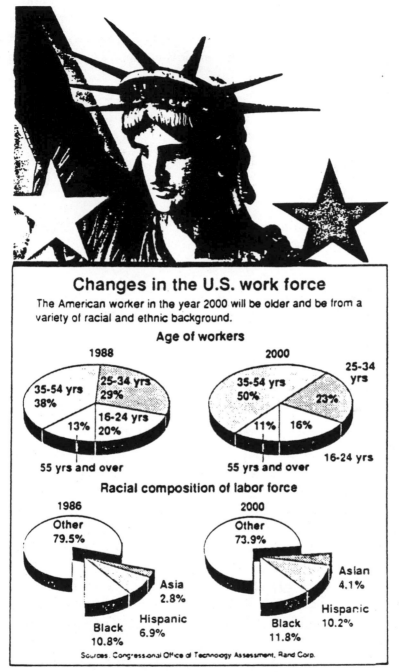

Changes in the U.S. work force

The American worker in the year 2000 will be older and be from a variety of racial and ethnic background.

Age of workers

1988

35-54 yrs 38%
25-34 yrs 29%
16-24 yrs 20%
13%
55 yrs and over

2000

35-54 yrs 50%
25-34 yrs
23%
11% 16%
55 yrs and over
16-24 yrs

Racial composition of labor force

1986

Other 79.5%
Asia 2.8%
Hispanic 6.9%
Black 10.8%

2000

Other 73.9%
Asian 4.1%
Hispanic 10.2%
Black 11.8%

Sources: Congressional Office of Technology Assessment. Rand Corp.

Bilingual Education Means Equal Opportunity

Figure 1.

students cluster together, discuss topics and learn to take charge of their own learning. They learn how to learn by participation with a broad range of peers in small group activities. Team spirit, rather than individual rivalry, is stressed as students develop ways of working together.

Collaborative knowledge building includes strategies for connecting thinking to cooperative group work. Students learn how to jointly search out information on questions generated by individuals or the group. They learn techniques for analyzing, interpreting, negotiating and communicating their information as a team. In cooperative learning the individual may be held accountable, but all students are encouraged to pool their talents to help each other learn.

The process seems to help a wide range of students. The exposure of less academically inclined students to a peer value system that values learning and studying improves everyone's school achievement.[8] In addition, the research suggests that when peer value systems take learning seriously, dropout rates and delinquency levels go down.[9] The same group process seems to assist the development of mature thinkers who are able to cooperate in the acquisition and use of knowledge.

COOPERATIVE LEARNING AND TOMORROW'S WORKPLACE

Why do we remember the past, and not the future?
—Stephen W. Hawking, *A Brief History of Time*

New technological work requirements are changing the educational equation at an accelerating rate. Study after study has shown that students today are ill served by the silent and frequently isolated teaching techniques formed in the days of isolated assembly lines. The old top-down organizational model has been replaced (in the world outside of school) by new concerns about collective responsibility.[10] Even normally competitive firms are realizing that they have to collaborate to progress through technological change cycles more quickly. To stay competitive in the world market, over a hundred consortiums have recently been formed in the United States. These involve col-

---

8. Slavin, R. (1983). *Cooperative Learning.* New York: Longman.

9. Levine, M. & Trachtman, R. (Eds.). (1988). *American Business and the Public School: Case Studies of Corporate Involvement in Public Education.* New York: Teachers College Press.

10. Kraft, R. G. (1985). Group inquiry turns passive students active. *College Teaching* 33, (4): 149–54.

lective arrangements between various industries, government agencies and universities—focusing on projects that are vital to our national economy.

New opportunities are arising from the cooperative control of knowledge that are directly connected to the level of human literacy and the ability to manipulate symbols. In the new workplace power is frequently shared and collaboration encouraged. Schools can adapt to this changing reality by shucking long-held educational models of teacher talk, textbook memorization and moving pupils from box to box with a bell. These are poor examples for future workers, professionals, and poets.

The Power of Metaphor

The ideas underlying how we structure schools come from our associations. In the 1970s and 1980s industrial analogies drove teaching, research and curriculum models in education. Dowdy rust belt metaphors influenced theory, practice and the design of research investigations. Terms like "time on task," "classroom management," "cost investment" and "student productivity" were all part of placing students in an educational version of a work setting where everyone was expected to proceed at the same pace through a similar task. This reflected a certain level of belief in "rational" absolutes that proved to be a subtle energy of mind standing in the way of equity and intellectual quality.

With a vocabulary drenched in yesteryear, teachers were held "accountable" and learning was viewed as secondary to maintaining the work system. Students were encouraged to work hard at homework, seatwork, schoolwork and student assessment was based on their work habits. In this context, teachers were viewed as supervisors (or managers) and students as assembly line workers. The best teachers, seeking a more professional voice in how their schools were run, often came into conflict with the "quality control" system of management.

Things in the "real world" have changed. Instead of just using arms and legs, industry is learning how to use the whole person. These fundamental organizational changes are supported by unions, management, and the public. There is nothing wrong with schools borrowing workplace metaphors—as long as they are up-to-date and accurate. Outdated associations, time, and progress as Margaret Atwood has suggested, are not straight lines . . .

but dimensions... a shape, something you can see, like a series of liquid transparencies, one laid on top of another. You don't look back along time, but down through it, like water. Sometimes this comes to the surface, sometimes that, sometimes nothing. Nothing goes away.

                                 —Cat's Eye

Even as new understandings invoke new images, few educational traditions, like individual competition, seem willing to simply go away.

Harnessing the Powerful Dynamics of Collaborative Learning

Educators are trying to redesign professional structures that have traditionally left teachers isolated from their colleagues. Fostering professional collaboration between respected professionals isn't easy. It is no easier to change a whole profession's view of the world, after its been in place for a long time, than it is to create a new social and economic environment. All is not gloom and doom, however. We do have some proven models that can positively shape schooling in the future. The school reform agenda for the 1990s is turning to look at shared management, how pupils are grouped and parental involvement. School and classroom organization are taking center stage as we approach a fundamental reordering of educational priorities.

    Economists tell us that about half of any nation's increase in productivity comes from the knowledge and skill growth of its population.[11] Educational levels certainly make a difference, but the quality of the organizational structure is also important. Companies have found that combining on-site learning centers with varying levels of collective responsibility improves productivity. Power-sharing models are proving better than their factory-floor predecessors. When people consider themselves part of the decision-making process and are encouraged to improve the system, they become more productive.[12]

    The basic elements of cooperation and higher level thinking skills are coming to be viewed as essential skills for today's workplace and tomorrow's workforce. As far as the schools are concerned, developing a high level of interpersonal and small group skills means going beyond ability grouping or individual assignments at the same table. Interdependence (in

---

11. Heseltine, M.: *The Challenge of Europe: Can Britain Win?.* Weidenfeld, 1989.

12. Oliver, D. & Gershman, K: *Education, Modernity and Fractured Meaning: Toward a Theory of Process Teaching and Learning.* The State University of New York Press, 1989.

tasks, resources, and rewards) is different from physical proximity. It also means more than having the faster students help the slower ones when their work is done. Cooperative learning places the emphasis on social solidarity and joint responsibility for reaching group goals.

When teachers emphasize interpersonal competition the result can be diminished accomplishment and alienation from school. When a student finds out that the only way to reach her personal objectives is by helping everyone in the group reach *their goal,* she is much more likely to seek outcomes beneficial to all. The building of a cooperative learning community can allow for collective and individual expression, even if part of the process is difficult. Encouraging higher levels of thinking, collective responsibility, and peer support for individual and team achievement are all key elements in building a cooperative learning framework.

BASING COLLABORATIVE LEARNING EFFORT
ON RELIABLE DATA

Studies have shown disadvantaged students significantly benefit from collaborative learning techniques.[13] And students who have always done well can reach higher levels of achievement as pupils with less information drive and motivate the students with more. By teaching others, all of the students can actually come to understand the material better.[14]

The research suggests that:

- Cooperative learning has been shown to improve academic performance among high and low achievement students.
- Consistently favorable achievement results have been made by minority students in cooperative classes.
- Forming mixed-ability groups into a unified learning community doesn't stifle individual initiative.
- Cooperative learning programs have been found to improve self-esteem, social relations, attitudes toward mainstreamed students and race relations.
- Children's cooperative behavior skills were shown to transfer to interaction with peers who weren't members of the same learning

13. Sharan, S. & Shachar, H. (1988). *Language and Learning in the Cooperative Classroom.* New York: Springer-Verlag.

14. Webb, N. M.: "Student Interaction and Learning In Small Groups," *Review of Educational Research,* 52, 1982, 421–445.

teams. It also transferred to their behavior in social situations not
structured by the teacher.
- Cooperative learning methods have proven to be practical and
  widely acceptable to teachers.
- Cooperative learning methods are often used by teachers to jointly
  achieve social and academic goals.[15,16]

Our survey research has found that when students are encouraged to
work collaboratively, there is a positive effect on the overall school
environment. This includes teachers becoming more cooperative in
their own professional interactions and more willing to collaborate with
their peers.[17] Attitudes that can affect the level of success include:
resistance, learning from failure, awareness of resource potential in the
environment, and striving to work up to and beyond personal limits.
Just as it is with students, the teacher's commitment to academic and
organizational tasks is a major determinant of their level of success.

How Group Support Can Help Students

*In our schools students are mostly trained to work alone and get the right
answers quickly. This can hamper collaboration, thinking and the sorely
needed ability to handle open-ended situations.*
—Sara Lawrence Lightfoot

The more options students have open to them, the more learning takes
on an element of ambiguity similar to today's world of work. Part of
teaching is helping students learn how to tolerate uncertainty and consider possibilities. Students may want answers when what they need are
ideas for thinking skills to grow on. Asking questions that are not fully
answerable exercises the imagination and furnishes it with important
intellectual values.

The peer-support structures that develop as students learn to work in
cooperative groups can help them deal with open-ended questions. The
small group provides opportunities for trial and error, as it provides a
safe environment for asking questions, expressing opinions, and taking
risks. In high-spirited teams more pupils get a chance to respond, raise

---

15. Slavin, R.: *School and Classroom Organization.* Hillsdale, NJ, Erlbaum, 1989.

16. Abraham, S.Y. & Campbell, C.: *Peer Teachers as Mirrors and Monitors.* Michigan: Wayne State University, 1984.

17. Adams, D. & Hamm, M.: *Media and Literacy.* Springfield, IL: Charles C Thomas, 1989.

issues or question ideas that are unclear. And since each student brings unique strengths and experiences to the group, respect for individual differences can be enhanced.[18]

Getting together in teams (to accomplish something) is a great motivator. Projects and ideas are frequently pushed beyond what an individual would attempt or suggest. The quality and quantity of thinking increases as more ideas are added, surpassing what the student could do alone. Group interaction enhances idea development, and students have many opportunities to be teachers as well as learners.

Simultaneously, the small group structure extends children's resources as they are encouraged to pool strategies and share information. More withdrawn students become more active. Students who often have a hard time sticking to a task receive group assistance so they can learn to monitor their time better and become a productive member of the group. This group unity has been found to extend beyond the classroom, to the playground and social situations.[19] We can hope that it will fuse the relationship between knowledge and the common welfare.

TEACHERS AS PROFESSIONAL COLLABORATORS

Creating conditions under which teachers can gain and sustain knowledge is as important as creating the conditions for an enriched learning environment. Shared curriculum development and decision making requires knowledgeable professionals (teachers) working in an environment that allows time for creative planning, research, risk-taking and thoughtful evaluation. Moving from the certainty of textbooks and teachers' manuals requires that teachers have a deep understanding of their subject matter, a thorough knowledge of the characteristics of effective instruction, and a chance to keep up-to-date. Teacher-renewal efforts are finding that a team approach helps overcome isolation while building networks to sustain teachers. If teachers can weather this period of collective retooling, there's hope that a renaissance, rather than a dark age, is in the offing. In the final analysis, any reform movement has to be

---

18. Meece, J. L. & Blumenfeld, P. C.: *Elementary School Children's Motivational Orientation and Patterns of Engagement in Classroom Activities.* Paper presented at American Educational Research Association, Washington, D.C., 1987.

19. Ziegler, S.: The Effectiveness of Cooperative Learning Teams for Increasing Cross Ethnic Friendship. *Human Organization,* 40, 1981, 264–68.

based on the individual teacher's commitment, expertise, and ability to continue learning.

To develop comfort with the fluid character of today's knowledge, the old model of teaching as filling empty vessels (students' minds) will have to be replaced with one that might be described as teaching as chore-ography or teaching as coaching. Getting students excited about a sub-ject and linking it personally to stimulation and meaning is an act of pedagogical leadership. When teachers take collective responsibility for how schools are managed and students take more responsibility for their own learning, a synergy of teaching and learning develops. Instead of rivalry in class, a team spirit can emerge that provides group support as students internalize ladders of knowledge and wrest personal meaning from the discipline.

New models for teaching and learning cannot be put in place without going beyond how considering overall school structure. Support for new learning strategies, school organizational patterns and the need for social changes are interwoven. Without political, social, and economic support, without a societal commitment to sustained support, it is difficult to talk about empowering teachers or improving the texture and richness of learning. Fortunately, we seem to be moving towards a societal consensus. The public and leaders in every field are coming to agree that starving our educational institutions will prevent the private sector retooling necessary for serving the needs of the 1990s and beyond. This means that school policies, structures, and curriculum are being pushed to keep up with a new world of work where people can work autonomously and effectively with others.[20]

The Role of the Teacher In the Cooperative Classroom

Once the curriculum of the past is viewed from a safe distance, it can be seen as a quaint anachronism, but while your professional life is squeezed into its narrow confines, the charm escapes you. Traditional goal structures tended to be teacher centered. Teachers controlled learn-ing by imparting knowledge, maintaining control, and validating thinking. Times have changed. The skills needed for the 1990s can only be achieved by teaching students to be self-starting thinkers who can work together to solve problems.

---

20. Wideen, M. & Andrews, I.: *Staff Development for School Improvement.* Philadelphia, Falmer, 1987.

Small-group cooperative learning involves significant changes in the role of the classroom teacher. In the cooperative learning classroom the teacher is faced with the difficult task of encouraging students to become responsible for their own learning. One of the goals is to have students rely more heavily upon their classmates for assistance in doing a task and evaluating an answer. Only after they have checked with everyone in the group can they ask the teacher for help. Teachers specify the instructional objectives, arrange the classroom to maximize social interaction, provide the appropriate materials, explain the task and the cooperative goal structure, observe the student interactions, and help students solve some of the more difficult problems. They pay attention to the learning process and social relationships within the groups. And they evaluate the group products.

In a collaborative setting the teacher helps children gain confidence in their own ability and the group's ability to work through problems and consequently rely less on the teacher as the sole knowledge source. Students are motivated more by the social contact with their peers and by their sense of achievement as they succeed in challenging tasks through the group effort rather than through strict, step-by-step, teacher direction.

Students in cooperative learning settings often raise questions and ideas which go beyond the teacher's guide. To keep up-to-date teachers must also continue being learners and become comfortable with saying "I don't know" or "let's find out" as students push them in new learning directions unimagined and unplanned. The better a student becomes at learning, the wider the repertoire of skills, strategies and capacity for selecting and combining these thinking skills as required by the process of learning.

Cooperative classroom environments will not materialize overnight without effort. Teachers need to understand and actively seek to create them. A conceptual reexamination of the organizational process and grouping structures is needed to form collaborative learning groups. When they do, many teachers will find that their best instincts about mixed-ability group work could have promoted better learning all along.

Teaching Advantages

Dividing the class into groups means the teacher has five, six or seven groups instead of 25 to 35 individuals to make good contact with each day. In addition, there are 25 to 35 aides in the classroom. Pupils monitor

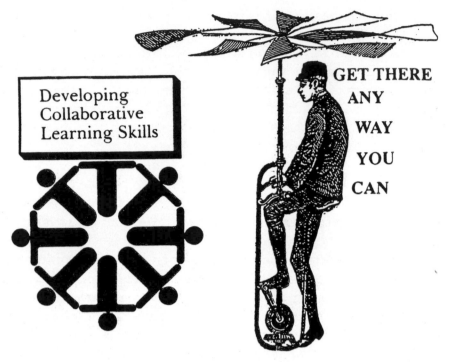

Figure 2.

each other while creating a spirit of cooperation and helpfulness. Students seem to become better listeners within a cooperative structure. If the group doesn't get to the bottom of an issue, they can collectively ask for the teacher's help. This way, they ask better questions, are more eager for teacher input, and collective answers can lead to more questions.

Cooperative learning can help teachers spend less time being policemen as students learn that they are capable of validating their own values and ideas. Teachers are freer to move about, work with small groups and interact in a more personal manner with students. Cooperative group learning can also be arranged so there is less paperwork for the teacher. Six or eight group papers is less than 24 or 32. In this structure teachers continue to be learners, opening new channels of thinking and learning.

The Student's Role Is Changing

Students must also undergo a major shift in values and attitudes if a collaborative learning environment is to succeed. Getting over years of learned helplessness will take time. The school experience has taught students that the teacher is there to validate their thinking and direct learning. Upon entering school, students have been constantly compared with one another for grades and recognition. For many, teacher's direction on the smallest detail becomes the order of the day. Students learn that it's easy to predict their success based on their past performance. Unlearning these dated modeling structures takes time.

It is important that students understand that simply "telling an answer" or "doing someone's work" is not helping a classmate learn. Lending assistance involves helping someone grasp the meaning or explaining with an example. These understandings need to be actively explained, demonstrated, and developed by the teacher. The role of the teacher in a new classroom setting is akin to a scientific researcher constantly testing hypotheses. They are the prime decision makers, professionals who must make thousands of decisions influenced by a whole range of complicating factors. To make this work, teachers must all be members of a community of learners who can work with colleagues to improve learning. Ways must be developed to drive decision making down to the people actually doing the teaching. To paraphrase an old parable, if educators aren't the ones "making the dust, they will be the ones eating it."

Attitudes also change as students learn to work cooperatively.[21] Rather than taking individual ownership of ideas, students share recognition. They learn to evaluate the learning outcomes rather than hurrying to finish the task. Small groups can write collective stories, edit each other's writing, solve mathematics problems, correct homework, prepare for tests, investigate science questions, examine artifacts, work on a computer simulation, brainstorm an invention, create a sculpture, or arrange a new rap music tune. Working together, students synthesize what they have learned, collaboratively present to a small group, coauthor a written summary or communicate the concept through the subtleties of the arts. Cooperative learning becomes more a "culture" or set of collaborative values (pervading the classroom) than a technique.

Within cooperative learning groups the student's role as collaborative researcher replaces the traditional notion of student as a passive knowledge recipient. Learning starts with curiosity, moves toward students' interpretation of the subject's meaning in their lives and is then connected to other areas of knowledge. Children learn by "talking out,"

---

21. Educational Researcher Editors: Cooperative learning: A research success story, *Educational Researcher,* 3, 1985.

assimilating ideas through group interaction, and assuming a higher level of responsibility for what they set out to learn. For Sartre, acting on social responsibility and freedom involved both "a rejection of the insufficient, an imaging of a better state or collective thing . . . a flight and a leap ahead in thinking, at once a refusal and a realization."[22]

REFERENCES

Abraham, S.Y. & Campbell, C.: *Peer Teachers as Mirrors and Monitors.* Michigan: Wayne State University, 1984.

Adams, D. & Hamm, M.: *Media and Literacy.* Springfield, IL: Charles C Thomas, 1989.

Armstrong, J. Paper presented at 1989 IBM Conference. New York.

Atwood, M.: *Cat's Eye.* New York: Doubleday, 1988.

Brophy, J. & Good, T.: Teacher behavior and student achievement. In M.C. Wittrock (Ed.) *Research on Teaching.* New York: St. Martin's Press, 1986.

DeVries, D. & Slavin, R.: Teams-games-tournaments (TGT): Review of ten classroom experiments. *Journal of Research and Development in Education, 12,* 1978, 28–38.

Dinkmeyer, D. & McKay, G. D.: *Systematic training for effective parenting.* Circle Pines, Minnesota: American Guidance Service, 1976.

Edelman, M.: *Families in Peril: An Agenda for Social Change.* Cambridge, Harvard University Press, 1989.

Education Commission of the States: *One Third of a Nation: A Report of the Commission on Minority Participation in Education and American Life.* Washington, D.C., American Council on Education, 1988.

Educational Researcher Editors.: Cooperative learning: A research success story. *Educational Researcher, 3,* 1985.

Gordon, T.: *P. E. T. Parent effectiveness training: The tested new way to raise responsible children.* New York: New American Library, 1970.

Gordon, T. with Burch, N.: *T. E. T. Teacher effectiveness training.* New York: David McKay Company, 1974.

Hawking, S.: *A Brief History of Time.* New York: Bantam, 1988.

Heseltine, M.: *The Challenge of Europe: Can Britain Win?* Weidenfeld, 1989.

Hertz-Lazarowtiz, R., Sharan, S. & Steinberg, R.: "Classroom learning styles of elementary school children." *J of Educ. Psychology,* 1980, 7299-106.

Hochschild, J.: *The New American Dilemma: Liberal Democracy and School Desegration.* New Haven, Yale University Press, 1984.

Holmes Group: *Forum,* 3 (1), Fall, 1988.

Johnson, D. & Johnson, R.: *Learning Together and Alone: Cooperation, Competition, and Individualization.* Englewood Cliffs, NJ, Prentice-Hall, 1974.

Johnson, D. W. Maruyama, G., Johnson, R., Nelson, D., & Skon, L.: "Effects of

---

22. Sartre, J.P. *Search for a Method.* New York, Alfred A. Knopf, 1963.

cooperative competitive, and individualistic goal structures on achievement: A meta analysis." *Psychological Bulletin*, 89, 1981, 47–62.

Kearns, D.: *Winning the Brain Race: A Bold Plan To Make Our Schools Competitive.* Institute for Contemporary Studies, 1987.

Kraft, R. G.: Group inquiry turns passive students active. *College Teaching*, 33, (4); 1985, 149–54.

Levine, M. & Trachtman, R. (Eds.): *American Business and the Public School: Case Studies of Corporate Involvement in Public Education.* New York: Teachers College Press, 1988.

Meece, J. L. & Blumenfeld, P. C.: *Elementary School Children's Motivational Orientation and Patterns of Engagement in Classroom Activities.* Paper presented at American Educational Research Association, Washington, D.C., 1987.

Newmann, F. M. & Thompson, J.: *Effects of cooperative learning on achievement in secondary schools: A summary of research.* Madison, WI: University of Wisconsin, National Center on Effective Secondary Schools, 1987.

Oliver, D. & Gershman, K.: *Education, Modernity and Fractured Meaning: Toward a Theory of Process Teaching and Learning.* The State University of New York Press, 1989.

Rubin, K. H. & Everett, B.: Social perspective-taking in young children. In S. G. Moore & C. R. Cooper (Eds), *The Young Child: Reviews of Research* (vol. 3). Washington, D.C.: National Association for the Education of Young Children, 1982.

Sartre, J.P.: *Search for a Method.* New York, Alfred A. Knopf, 1963.

Sharon, S.: Cooperative learning in small groups: Recent methods and effects on achievement, attitudes and ethnic relations. *Review of Educational Research*, 50, 1980, 241–271.

Sharan, S. & Shachar, H.: *Language and Learning in the Cooperative Classroom.* New York: Springer-Verlag, 1988.

Slavin, R.: *Cooperative Learning.* New York: Longman, 1983.

Slavin, R.: *School and Classroom Organization.* Hillsdale, NJ: Erlbaum, 1989.

Slavin, R.: Cooperative learning and student achievement. *Educational Leadership*, 54, 1988, 31–33.

Webb, N.M.: "Student Interaction and Learning in Small Groups." *Review of Educational Research*, 52, 1982, 421–445.

Ziegler, S.: The effectiveness of cooperative learning teams for increasing cross-ethnic friendship. *Human Organization*, 40, 1981, 264–268.

2

STRUCTURING COOPERATIVE LEARNING: STRATEGIES FOR WORKING TOGETHER AS A COMMUNITY OF LEARNERS

There is a profound principle of learning here:
we can learn to do alone what at first we could do only with others.
— P. Elbow

New organizational models can help teachers apply cooperative curriculum constructs in their classrooms. As they organize interactive learning environments children learn to shape questions, interpret data, and make connections between subjects. When small learning groups are formed, under teacher direction, students can learn to take responsibility for their own learning and assist others. This means collaboration instead of competition. It exemplifies an approach where task-oriented work groups combine student initiative with social responsibility. Thus, students with less information can stimulate the students with more—and vice versa. The same thing is true when it comes to teaching thinking process like comprehension, decision making, and problem solving.[1]

Various heterogeneous group structures can help students set personal learning agendas. They can also provide the structure for the joint application of critical thinking skills—distinguishing hypotheses from verified information and recognizing reasoning based on misconceptions. Cooperative groups invite students to be active players in classroom activities. Topical projects, writing assignments, problem solving or journal reaction papers are examples of activities that require group planning, negotiating and the collaborative distribution of work. Group activities can be brought to closure by forming a panel or round table. As groups try to reach consensus they can create an analysis grid whereby comparisons and contrasts can be made as well as students' speculations

---

1. Kuhn, D.. Amsel, E. & O'Loughlin, M.: *The Development of Scientific Thinking Skills.* San Diego, Academic Press, 1988.

20

about outcomes. Within the tension of discussing different points of view (even heated discussion), learning takes place.

Establishing the classroom conditions for the successful use of cooperative learning means more than having educators decide that it is an appropriate organizational method for enhancing learning. Students must also develop collaborative skills for mixed-ability pairs or groups to work productively. This chapter identifies some guidelines that have proven successful in helping students and teachers develop and structure cooperative learning.

Organizing the Collaborative Classroom

Cooperative learning will not take place with students sitting in rows facing the teacher. Desks must be pushed together in small groups or replaced with small tables to facilitate group interaction. Resource and hands-on materials must be made readily accessible. Collaboration will not occur in a classroom which requires students to raise their hands to talk or move out of their desks. Responsible behavior needs to be developed and encouraged. Authoritarian approaches to discipline will not work if students are expected to be responsible for their own learning and behavior.

Other changes involve the noise level in the room. Sharing and working together even in controlled environments will be louder than an environment where students work silently from textbooks. Teachers need to tolerate higher noise levels and learn to evaluate whether or not it's constructive.

Evaluating cooperative learning necessitates a variety of procedures. In spite of new evaluative techniques on the horizon, some learning outcomes will probably continue to be measured by such instruments as standardized tests, quizzes, and written exams. In addition, cooperative learning demands subjective measures. Students and teachers need to be involved in evaluating learning products, the classroom climate, and individual skill development. This involves such things as self-esteem, discipline, cooperation, values, expression, individual and group achievement.

Changes In the Learning Environment

Researchers who are concerned with the inequality of learning possibilities fostered by traditional classroom organization suggest that we should reduce the general preoccupation with competition and ability grouping.[2] Cooperative learning would also appear to have a natural role to play in overcoming the suppression of human aspirations that have played such a central role in competitive tracking models.

Model schools can help, but major change will require an emphasis on visions and a sizable national experiment. As the United States runs out of workers who are even minimally prepared to do the jobs of the 1990s, the problem of improving the educational system becomes even more urgent. There are important factors schools must consider if this learning model is to be successfully implemented in schools. Changing classroom organizational patterns and teaching strategies requires systematic staff development and the association of like-minded colleagues. It also takes time, practice, and systematic support for the vital energy inherent in new skills to become part of teachers' repertoire.

The traditional system of school and classroom organization is no longer enough. There is general agreement that it will take more than tinkering to get the job done. Major change will require educational vision and greater societal commitments than we have seen to date. It's a question of knowledgeable educators and social priorities. The public tends to put its wallet where its values are. Even when values change, it takes time for victimized institutions—like schools—to catch up. And, although it sets a positive tone of concern, fragmentary private or corporate efforts barely dent the problem. Some are even a kind of hit-and-run socio-educational effort with no follow through.

No matter what the collaborative combinations, educators are not on the margins of meaningful and systemic educational change. Encouraging participation in decisions affecting the workplace is a key element in developing new schools. If teachers aren't part of the process, then they will be part of an unsolvable problem. They must be recognized as knowledgeable professionals who are capable of assuming even greater responsibility for how schools and classrooms are organized. Teachers actively involved in learning the most efficient strategies and goal structures need support while implementing new skills.

Change takes resources, time and practice for the vital energy inherent in new skills to become part of a teacher's repertoire. Management studies suggest that the best way to improve job satisfaction, a major

---

2. Jussim, L.: Self-fulfilling Prophecies: A Theoretical and Integrative Review. *Psychological Review,* 93, 1986, 429–445.

cause of teacher attrition, is to attain a high group performance.[3] In-service workshops can help provide assistance as teachers try activities and share experiences. But, in the final analysis, they need to give and receive feedback from colleagues within a structure that supports collaboration.

Changes in the organization of learning requires an environment where it is safe to make mistakes and where it is safe to learn from those mistakes. Social interaction, creativity, inventiveness, discovery and critical thinking are crucial ingredients that must be applied to the collaborative learning process. Like any other proven method, cooperative learning is only as good as the ability of its practitioners to model the behavior. For the teacher, the best way to deal with team spirit in the classroom is to join in.

Aids To Collaborative Learning

Research suggests that:

- Collaboration works best when students are given real problems to solve.
- A collaborative environment grows slowly nurtured by teachers who consider everyone a resource.
- Learning to think as a team that "sinks or swims" together can help many students learn more.
- A collaborative environment works best if it allows risks and mistakes.
- Collaborative learning allows practice in solving problems.
- Individuals learn best when they are held individually responsible for group subtasks.
- The less academically talented develop better learning attitudes when they work directly with "successful" students.
- Roles often change; student as tutor or teacher—and teacher as learner.[4]

3. Sansone, C. "A Question of Competence: The Effects of Competence and Task Feedback on Intrinsic Interest," *Journal of Personality and Social Psychology*, 51, 1986.

4. Hord, S., Rutherford, W., Huling-Austin, L., & Hall, G.: *Taking Charge of Change*. Alexandria, VA, Association for Supervision and Curriculum Development, 1987.

Suggestions for Small Group Collaboration

- Adjust the group size to suit the activity. Groups of 3 or 4 work well for many activities like mathematics problem solving. Groups of 5 to 7 work better for activities that require larger group participation or more complicated (creative dramatics, larger social studies projects, certain writing projects, etc.).
- Accept a higher working noise level in the classroom.
- Do not interrupt a group that is working well. If a group seems to be floundering, ask a student to describe what the group is discussing or what part of the problem is causing difficulty. Try not to speak loudly to a group across the room. Go to them if you want to say something.
- Experiment with different group patterns and size.
- Try interacting with the groups from time to time. *Listen* to their discussions.
- Give students rules for group work. Some suggestions:
  - Individuals must check with other members of the group before they may raise their hands to ask the teacher for help. Help can then be given to the group collectively.
  - Try to reach a group consensus on a problem.
  - All students should participate.
  - Be considerate of others.
  - Students are to help any group member who asks.
- Promote involvement by all students
  - Select a group leader to be responsible for the group's work.
  - Identify a recorder to write group's responses.
  - Encourage students who do not appear to be actively participating.

COOPERATIVE LEARNING:
CIVIC VIRTUE AND LEARNING COMMUNITIES

Collective genius has reigned supreme in fields as diverse as the physical and social sciences for the last fifty years—from the development of the atomic bomb, to macro economic theory, to cognitive stages of human development. However, connecting positive social values to accomplishment is like confusing virtue with talent. It takes more than academic skills to be a good citizen. Beyond the discussions of academic achievement, economic competitiveness and technology lay concerns with personal freedom and a sense of being part of a social unit.

Developing a sense of connectedness and feelings of common membership in a civic community has always been a function of American education. Our schools are receiving a growing number of students from countries with no democratic tradition of concern for the common good, public service, or active participation in governance. Other students are stuck in an underclass and groping for equity. Educators are searching for ways to help this growing number of non-traditional pupils create and expand civic sensibilities.

Cooperative learning may be able to help us on several social and academic fronts. Numerous studies have shown significant student gains on measures of achievement, measures of social relationships, self-esteem, and cross-cultural relationships.[5,6] These well-documented benefits are causing educators to reexamine their assumptions about classroom grouping. Organizing environments for learning that allow students to explore and connect the links between civics and cooperative groups helps prepare the young for citizenship.[7]

The ways we choose to spend our teaching/learning time conveys implicit messages to students about what is valued and important. If most of the time is spent listening to the teacher or working on isolated paper-and-pencil tasks, the underlying concept conveyed is that learning means mastering a narrow range of skills that are found mainly in textbooks or on practice sheets. Important educational matters are—and have always been—much broader; more an attitude toward learning and the world than a set of subskills.

COOPERATIVE LEARNING SKILLS

It often takes several attempts with cooperative learning techniques to get groups working effectively. Like teachers, students must be gradually eased into the process through a consistent routine. The more teachers and students work in groups, the easier it becomes. Some students may encounter initial problems because they are accustomed to being rewarded

5. Slavin, R.E.: *School and Classroom Organization*. Hillsdale, NJ, Erlbaum, 1989.

6. Sharan & Shachar: *Language Learning in the Cooperative Classroom*. New York, Springer-Verlag, 1988.

7. Pratte, R.: *The Civic Imperative: Examining the Need for Civic Education*. New York, Teachers College Press, 1989.

for easy-to-come-by answers that require little thinking. It may take some time and teacher assistance for them to become comfortable working cooperatively with more ambiguity.

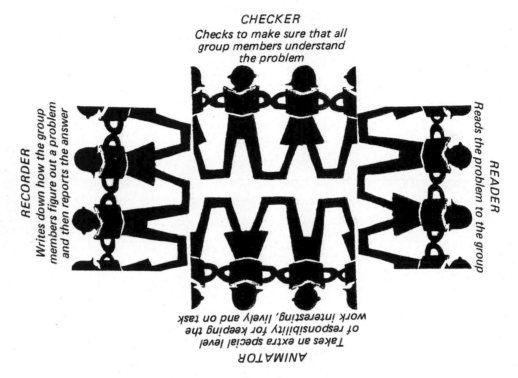

Figure 3.

Shared Responsibility and Group Roles

Collaborative group structures involve shared responsibilities. This means that a variety of tasks must be performed by group members. Each member of a group assumes the charge of making sure that group members work toward a group goal or objective. When students are new to cooperative learning and during some initial experiences, teachers may wish to assign certain roles to group participants. Some of the most frequent group tasks include:

1. Facilitator
   - organizes the group's work
   - makes certain students understand the group's job

- takes the group's questions and concerns to the teacher *after* the group attempts a solution and tries alternatives.
2. Checker
    - checks with group members to make sure that everyone understands their task
    - checks to be sure that everyone agrees with the group response and can explain it.
3. Reader
    - reads the problem or directions to the group
4. Recorder
    - writes the group's response or data collection on a group response sheet or log.
5. Encourager
    - offers support and encouragement to group members. Keeps others feeling good about working together.

All students assume responsibility for promoting and maintaining positive attitudes and a positive group spirit. This doesn't mean using the "team spirit" to suppress dissent or intimidate individuals.

All of these responsibilities involve specific skills and behaviors:

1. *Clarifying and elaborating* — interpreting information or building on information from another group member.
2. *Providing information or giving opinions* — sharing relevant knowledge and ideas with the group
3. *Seeking facts, data, or opinions from group members* — searching out and requesting relevant information
4. *Summarizing* — recapitulating and pulling together the groups's shared knowledge and information
5. *Guiding and Managing* — establishing a process which helps the group achieve its goal or learning objective.

Organizing a group plan of action is an important part of shared responsibility and shared leadership. Learning how to search out, share and receive information to continue progress on a group task are important skills in working collaboratively. Students also need to learn how to summarize and clarify that information so as to move the group in the direction of completing their task or goal. Sometimes it may be necessary to test the consensus of a group—how many members agree that a particular direction is advisable or that a particular conclusion is accurate. Other task behaviors include:

- getting the group started
- staying on task
- getting the group back to work
- taking turns
- asking questions
- following directions
- staying in the group space
- keeping track of time
- helping without giving the answer

Group Support Systems

In addition to helping the group reach its goal and get the job done, a group member also has the responsibility to show support and empathy for other group members and their feelings. It is important to reflect on the group process and the feelings group members express. This assures that individual group members have opportunities to express ideas and opinions. When group interactions become tense, a release of that tension is needed; perhaps a funny joke will ease members' frustrations. Harmony can often be achieved when a group member acknowledges that another group member is upset.

Support or maintenance behaviors include the skills of:

1. *Compromising*—coming to an agreement by meeting halfway, "giving in" to other group members when necessary
2. *Empathizing and encouraging*—showing understanding and helping others feel a part of the group
3. *Gatekeeping*—giving everyone a chance to speak in the group, checking to see that no one is overlooked.
4. *Liberating tension*—creating harmony in the group
5. *Expressing group feelings*—helping the group to examine how it is feeling and operating

Other support or maintenance behaviors include:

- using names
- encouraging others to talk
- responding to ideas
- using eye contact
- showing appreciation
- disagreeing in a pleasant way

- criticizing an idea, not a person
- keeping things cool
- paraphrasing

It is helpful for groups to evaluate the effectiveness of each group meeting as soon as it is over. This provides feedback and insights into the collaborative process. As the group members learn to focus energy on the learning task, they also learn to identify with the group process—helping members grow and develop. Compromising, creating harmony, sharing and encouraging are learned behaviors. They take time, coaching, and commitment. When group responsibility and support behaviors are in balance, group members can work collaboratively to achieve important group objectives

Suggestions for Group Evaluation and Processing

1. How did your group get started on its task?
2. Did your group do something different from other groups?
3. Did your group approach the problem or task effectively?
4. How did your group reach agreement on your answer?
5. Are you satisfied with the way your group recorded the information? Would you do it differently next time?
6. How did working in a group help you?
7. What helped your group stick to its task?
8. How did you feel working in this group?
9. How did you offer support to other members of the group?
10. How did your group share information and ideas?
11. Which social skill will your group use more of next time?
12. Did your group accomplish its tasks? What did you learn?

Individualized, Competitive, and Cooperative Learning Methods

The team learning structure plays an important role in the group's ability to interact effectively. The most common structures in use are: individualized learning, competitive learning, and, increasingly, *cooperative learning*. Teachers are starting to reorder the priorities as they learn to place more emphasis on active group work.

Individualized Learning

In individualized learning structures, each student works at his own pace and expects to be left alone by other students. The individual takes a major part of the responsibility for completing the task, evaluating his progress toward task completion and the quality of his effort. The goal or task objective is perceived as important for each student, and each student expects to achieve the goal. Types of instructional activities center around specific skill and knowledge acquisition. The assignment is clearly defined and behavior is specified to avoid confusion and the need for extra help. The teacher is the major source for assistance, support and reinforcement.

Competitive Learning

When competitive goal structures exist, the goal is not perceived to be of large importance to the students and they can accept either winning or losing. Each student expects to have an equal chance to enjoy the activity (win or lose). Students monitor the progress of their competitors and compare ability, skills and knowledge with peers. Instructional activities tend to focus on skill practice, knowledge recall, and review. The assignments is clear with rules for competing specified. The teacher is the major resource and often directs the competitive activity.

Cooperative Learning

In a cooperative learning situation the goal is perceived as important for each student and students expect the group to achieve the goal. Each student expects positive interaction with other students, sharing of ideas and materials. Each group member is responsible for a particular task and accountable for her own knowledge or her own area of contribution to the group. All group members are expected to contribute to the group effort, dividing the tasks among them to capitalize on the diversity. Students receive support for risk taking, and all are expected to make contributions to the group effort. Other students are perceived to be the major source for assistance, support, and reinforcement.

Solving Problems and Resolving Conflict

The ability to solve problems and smoothly resolve conflict in the group are important tasks of cooperation and collaboration. When conflict arises, group members often take unyielding stances and refuse to consider other points of view. Groups members need strategies for negotiating and problem solving to successfully defuse conflict and create harmony. Some conflict strategies include:

1. *Withdrawal* — the individual withdraws from interaction, recognizing that the goal and the interaction are not important enough to be in conflict over.
2. *Forcing* — the task is more important than the relationship; members use all their energy to get the task done.
3. *Smoothing* — the relationship is more important than the task. Individuals want to be liked and accepted.
4. *Compromising* — the task and the relationship are both important, but there is a lack of time. Both members gain something and lose something.
5. *Confrontation* — Task and relationship are equally important; the conflict is defined as a problem-solving situation.[8]

Problem solving is a useful group strategy to assist in conflict resolution. This systematic five-step process of constructively addressing conflicts includes:

1. Defining the problem and its causes.
2. Generating alternative solutions to the problem.
3. Examining advantages and disadvantages to each alternative.
4. Deciding upon and implementing the most desirable solution.
5. Evaluating whether the solutions solve the problem.

Group members must define exactly what the problem is. On occasion, this can be difficult, but it is worth the effort. Once the problem is defined, group members can then suggest alternative solutions for the problem and explore the consequences of each of those alternatives. The group members then make a decision to try an alternative and to review the results within a stipulated period of time.[9] It's important to teach confrontation skills and techniques for successful resolution. Some of these include:

1. Describe behavior; do not evaluate, label, accuse or insult.
2. Define the conflict as a mutual problem, not a win-lose situation.

---

8. Johnson, D. & Johnson, F.: *Learning Together and Alone*. Englewood Cliffs, NJ, Prentice-Hall, 1975.

9. Eagen, G. (1986). *The skilled helper: A systematic approach to effective helping*. Belmont, California: Wadsworth.

3. Use "I" statements.
4. Communicate what you think and feel.
5. Be critical of ideas, not people; affirm other's competence.
6. Give everyone a chance to be heard.
7. Follow the guidelines for rational argument.
8. Make sure there is enough time for discussion.
9. Take the other person's perspective.[10]

Negotiating is also a learning part of problem resolution. It involves mutual discussion and arrangement of the terms of an agreement. The process of learning to "read" another's behavior for clues as to a problem solution is crucial in being able to guess what will appeal to another person and how to make a deal in which each participant's preferences or needs are considered.

Complementing the task and support behaviors are such communication skills as active listening. This means both attending to and responding to group and individual efforts. Active listening allows all group members to be fully in tune with each other. Acknowledging the content, feelings, or meaning of what another person is communicating lends itself to goodwill and understanding. Gatekeeping (giving everyone a chance to express their ideas) assures that all members of the group participate and are secure in the knowledge that they are contributing to the group.[11]

COOPERATIVE LEARNING APPROACHES

Programs can vary in terms of both task structures and reward contingencies. Four different cooperative learning methods have been extensively developed and researched. The Teams-Games-Tournaments (TGT) and the Student Teams and Achievement Divisions (STAD) are two general methods adaptable to most subject matter and grade levels. Team Assisted Instruction (TAI) and Cooperative Integrated Reading and Composition (CIRC) are designed for specific curricula and grade levels. All methods incorporate concepts of individual accountability, team rewards and equal opportunities for success, but approaches differ.

---

10. *The Friendly Classroom for a Small Planet: Collected Activities, Workshop Plans, and Songs that Teach Skill in Cooperation and Conflict Resolution.* Santa Cruz, CA, New Society Publishers.

11. Stanford, B. (Ed.): *Peacemaking: A Guide To Conflict Resolution for Individuals, Groups and Nations.* New York, Bantam, 1976.

In the STAD and TGT approaches new material is first presented by the teacher to the whole class. Following this initial presentation, pupils are organized into mixed-ability learning teams. Students work within their teams to ensure that all members have mastered the lesson objectives. In the Student Teams Achievement Division approach students take individual quizzes on the material, whereas in the Teams-Games-Tournaments method group members are asked questions orally in tournaments with other teams. This team competition involves three tournament tables where students of similar abilities from different teams accumulate points for their team. In both cases, scores are kept for both individuals and teams or groups.

Other cooperative methods include the Jigsaw approach, where a different portion of a learning task is completed by each group member. This entails mutual cooperation. For example, pupils within one group might be required to read a certain text, with each group member assigned a particular portion of that text. Each pupil becomes an expert for that certain section, although all pupils must pass a test on the entire passage. Often, the "experts" from different groups meet to discuss material before returning to their home groups to present and discuss their assigned material. Positive effects on both achievement, particularly for minority children, and cross ethnic friendships have resulted.[12,13] The research on the effects of cooperative learning also suggest:

- Positive effects on academic achievement measures:
  - improved performance on vocabulary tests
  - higher achievement scores on tests, mathematics computation and problem solving
- Improvement on interpersonal measures
  - mutual concern
  - friendships between pupils of different races and ability levels
- Improved attitudes:
  - toward school
  - students' perceptions of peer support for their own performances and self-esteem.[14]

---

12. Ziegler, S.: The Effectiveness of Cooperative Learning Teams for Increasing Cross-ethnic Friendship. *Human Organization*, 40, 1981, 241–71.

13. Sharon, S.: "Cooperative Learning In Small Groups: Recent Methods and Effects on Achievement, Attitudes and Ethnic Relations. *Review of Educational Research*, 50, 1980, 241–271.

14. Stallings, J. & Stipek, D.: Research on Early Childhood and Elementary School Teaching Programs. In Wittrock (Ed.), *Handbook of Research on Teaching and Learning*, 1986.

Student Teams-Achievement Divisions (STAD)

When using STAD , students are assigned to four-member learning teams that are mixed in performance level, sex, and ethnicity. After the teacher presents a lesson, students work within their teams to make sure that all members have mastered the lesson.

Cooperative Integrated Reading and Composition (CIRC)

The newest of the Student Team Learning methods is a comprehensive program for teaching reading and writing in the upper elementary grades called Cooperative Integrated Reading and Composition, or CIRC.

Jigsaw

In the Jigsaw method, students are assigned to six-member teams to work on academic material that has been broken down into sections.

Teams-Games-Tournament (TGT)

Using the same teacher presentations and teamwork as Student Teams-Achievement Divisions, TGT replaces the quizzes with weekly tournaments in which students compete with members of other teams to contribute points to their team scores.

Figure 4.

A Vision of the Future

*Time present and time past are both perhaps present
in time future. And time future in time past.*
— T. S. Eliot

There is ample evidence, from management and educational studies, to support the implementation of cooperative groups structures in the classroom. Still, the hierarchical model that some schools follow does not provide for cooperative teacher planning or for collaborative student activities. School districts are slow to pick up on the notion that greater productivity can occur when a professional "team spirit" — and a collective feeling of self-worth — is actively encouraged.

With current school practices being judged as inadequate, companies are moving to do their own training in social *and* basic skills. Corporate success in late twentieth century is coming to be equated with getting well-educated workers and giving them a sense of collective responsibility. Like its European and Japanese competitors, American companies are shedding top-down management styles for participatory work teams — with elements of decision making driven down to the lowest employee levels.

It is well to keep in mind that there is a difference between corporations and schools. There are many elements of schooling that go well beyond producing skilled workers. The schools do not — or at least should not — operate in a social vacuum. If the emphasis on cooperative groups works well for industry, elements of this type of organization can also become a more effective form of school and classroom structure for accelerating student achievement.

The responsibility for achieving excellence and opportunity in education will require new forms of collaboration by many institutional sectors of society. All will have to accommodate diverse cultural and learning styles. Major responsibilities in the future will be shared by schools, students, families, corporations, and governmental agencies. Support from all directions will be necessary if new organizational models in education are to avoid being wiped out in the name of "fiscal responsibility." We would all do well to remember that investing in a future rich with promise for our nation and our children represents the *most responsible use of limited funds.*

We would do well to remember that global competition has left behind regions that have relied on a relatively unskilled, undereducated workforce.

Many have found to their chagrin a major difference between short-term economic growth and long-term economic development. Development requires a strong educational base and a long-term commitment.

It's out of a crisis much like the educational one we are facing today that positive change often comes. Being concerned with education also means being concerned with preparing the ground for what is to come, even if we don't fully understand the possibilities. In joking about optimism in preparing for an uncertain future, Theodore Sorensen tells the story of a newcomer to Washington taking a taxi from the airport to downtown. On the way the tourist sees an engraving on a government building: *The Past Is Prologue.* When he asks the driver what it means, the taxi driver profoundly replies *"It means you ain't seen nothing yet."*

REFERENCES

Carkhuff, R. (1985). *The art of helping: Trainer's guide.* Amherst, Massachusetts: Human Resource Development Press.

Eagen, G. (1986). *The skilled helper: A systematic approach to effective helping.* Belmont, California: Wadsworth.

Filley, A. C. (1975). *Interpersonal conflict resolution.* Glenview, Illinois: Scott Foresman.

Good, T. L. & Brophy, J. (1989) "Teaching the Lesson." In R. Slavin (Ed.), *School and Classroom Organization.* Hillsdale, NJ: Lawrence Erlbaum Assoc.

Haines, D. B. & McKeachie, W. J. (1967) "Cooperation Verses Competitive Discussion Methods." *Journal of Educational Psychology,* 58, 386–90.

Hertz-Lazarowtiz, R., Sharan, S. & Steinberg, R. (1980). "Classroom learning styles of elementary school children." *J of Educ. Psychology,* 7299-106.

Hord, S., Rutherford, W., Huling-Austin, L., & Hall, G.: *Taking Charge of Change.* Alexandria, VA, Association for Supervision and Curriculum Development, 1987.

Johnson, D. W. & Johnson, R. T. (1974). *Learning together and alone: Cooperation, competition, and individualization.* Englewood Cliffs, New Jersey: Prentice-Hall.

Johnson, D. & Johnson, F.: *Learning Together and Alone.* Englewood Cliffs, NJ, Prentice-Hall, 1975.

Jussim, L. (1986). Self-fulfilling prophecies: A theoretical and integrative review. *Psychological Review,* 93:429–445.

Kraft, R. G. (1985). Group inquiry turns passive students active. *College Teaching,* 33, (4): 149–54.

Kuhn, D., Amsel, E. & O'Loughlin, M.: *The Development of Scientific Thinking Skills.* San Diego, Academic Press, 1988.

New Society Publishers: *The Friendly Classroom for a Small Planet: Collected Activities, Workshop Plans, and Songs that Teach Skill in Cooperation and Conflict Resolution.* Santa Cruz, CA, New Society Publishers.

Pratte, R.: *The Civic Imperative: Examining the Need for Civic Education.* New York, Teachers College Press, 1989.

Sansone, C. "A Question of Competence: The Effects of Competence and Task Feedback on Intrinsic Interest," *Journal of Personality and Social Psychology,* 51, 1986.

Sharon, S. (1980). Cooperative learning in small groups: Recent methods and effects on achievement, attitudes and ethnic relations. *Review of Educational Research,* 50, 241–271.

Sharan, S. & Shachar, H. (1988). *Language and Learning in the Cooperative Classroom.* New York: Springer-Verlag.

Slavin, R.E. (1989). *School and Classroom Organization.* Hillsdale, NJ: Erlbaum.

Spivack, G., Platt, J. & Shure, M. (1976). *The problem solving approach to adjustment.* San Francisco: Jossey-Bass.

Stallings, J. & Stipek, D. (1986). Research on early childhood and elementary school teaching programs. In M. Wittrock, *Handbook of Research on Teaching and Learning.*

Stanford, B. (Ed.). (1976). *Peacemaking: A guide to conflict resolution for individuals, groups, and nations.* New York: Bantam.

Webb, N.M. (1982), "Student Interaction and Learning in Small Groups." *Review of Educational Research,* 52: 421–445.

Ziegler, S. (1981). The effectiveness of cooperative learning teams for increasing cross-ethnic friendship. Additional evidence. *Human Organization,* 40, 264–268.

3

CRITICAL THINKING, COLLABORATION AND CITIZENSHIP: INVENTING A FRAMEWORK APPROPRIATE FOR OUR TIMES

What is most missed isn't something that's gone,
but something that will never happen.
— Margaret Atwood, Cat's Eye

It is generally agreed that traditional patterns of instruction and school organization do not assist in helping students learn how to think critically and develop good interpersonal skills. This popular belief is supported by several national surveys and reports suggesting that today's students have difficulty cooperating, thinking critically, dealing with innovations, and skillfully solving problems.[1,2]

Teachers are turning to cooperative learning groups to help students learn to work and think problems through together. Active involvement is the key to stimulating thinking about a subject. One of the goals of this collaborative interaction is to change how students view their own learning. Within this framework teachers and students are viewed as being able to generate knowledge worthy of communicating.

While there is agreement that growth in thinking and interpersonal skills is important, there is confusion about programs and approaches. Part of the problem is figuring out what we mean by critical thinking and collaboration. Educators have yet to settle the disagreement over whether or not critical thinking should be taught separately or integrated into core subjects in the curriculum. There is reliable data to support the two positions.[3] Rather than trying to resolve this issue, we leave the options open and provide suggestions for doing both.

---

1. National Assessment of Educational Progress, Washington, D.C., 1988.

2. Burns, M.: Teaching "what to do in arithmetic vs. teaching "what to do and why." *Educational Leadership,* 43, 34–38, 1986.

3. Baron, J.B. & Sternberg, R. J. (Eds.). *Teaching Thinking Skills: Theory and Practice.* New York, Freeman, 1987.

38

Critical thinking involves the ability to raise powerful questions about what's being read, viewed or listened to. As Perkins and others have suggested, effective problem solving, solid decision making, and insightful creations form the core structure of effective thinking and learning.[4] Developing mature thinkers who are able to acquire and use knowledge means educating minds rather than training memories.

Critical thinking and collaborative problem solving do not magically occur in a solitary vacuum. Instant-success formulas are not much help either. Thinking and interpersonal skills must be earned the old-fashioned way: by teaching and practice. But once learned, they have an edge that cuts deeply and isn't blunted easily.

Developing Collaboration and Critical Thinking Skills

Failure to develop certain thinking and group skills shows up in basic skill learning and the ability to continue to learn as adult workers (Wurman, 1989). It also influences the ability to deal with the widening gap between data, knowledge, and the motivation to continue learning. Commitment and effort applied to academic tasks are major factors in successful thinking. Good thinking, sound decision making, problem solving, and invention usually depends on a combination of deep subject matter expertise and general strategic knowledge.

The synthesis of thinking skill development and cooperative learning can have a major effect on all of these cognitive structures.[5] The fundamental search for meaning is part of the development of interpersonal abilities and thinking skills. Toward this end students work together actively to integrate new information with existing knowledge, select what is important, think strategically, and learn to make inferences beyond the information given. The methodolog cal elements are available. What's missing from the equation are new organizational structures for schools and classrooms.

National surveys go beyond indicating that schools are not doing a good job of fostering thinking skills.[6] They point out that school organization plays a major role in inhibiting critical and creative

---

4. Perkins, D. & Solomon, G. (1987). *Thinking: International Conference.* Hillsdale, NJ, Lawrence Erlbaum Associates.

5. Resnick, L.: *Education and Learning to Think.* Washington, D.C., Academy Press, 1987.

6. National Assessment of Educational Progress, Washington, D.C., 1988.

thinking.[7] Logistics, they find, take more time than quality instruction. Students are seldom asked for their opinions—nor are they encouraged to question each other, the teacher, or the textbook. Rarely are higher level questions raised or students asked to supply evidence to support their view. Much of this practice is due to the traditional way schooling has been viewed.

Traditional schoolwork has focused on the individual thinking and working alone. Work, personal life, and recreation usually involves other people. This lack of connection is proving to be an increasingly troublesome problem. American schools have traditionally emphasized passive learning—while learning in life takes place within active social systems. Success in school involves a narrow range of abstract thought. Success in life outside of school is more dependent on cognitive tools like computers, calculators, and the collaborative ability to ferret out bits of resource information when it's needed. Interactions between specialized skills, general knowledge, and interpersonal abilities are crucial.

Thinking Processes

Thinking processes are the fundamental dimensions of thinking; essential tools for achieving many objectives in the real world. Major thinking processes have been identified as:

- *Concept Formation* —establishing essential mental constructs
- *Principle Formation* —making generalizations that describe relationships which can be applied to multiple examples.
- *Comprehension* —extracting new information from a variety of sources and integrating it with what is already known.
- *Problem Solving* —step-by-step process of arriving at an unknown solution or solving a dilemma.
- *Decision Making* —choosing or inventing the best alternative based on some criteria.
- *Scientific Inquiry* —describing phenomena, formulating hypotheses, testing hypotheses, explaining, predicting.
- *Composition* —creating and developing a product.
- *Oral Discourse* —verbal interaction, inventive dialogue between two or more people.[8]

---

7. Goodlad, J.I. (1984). *A Place Called School.* New York: McGraw-Hill.

8. Grant, Wiggins: Creating a thought provoking curriculum. *American Educator,* Winter, 1987.

When it comes to designing today's curriculum, settling for the familiar isn't good enough. It is now necessary to infuse the thinking skill concepts—in addition to identifying the basic principles students must learn to comprehend the subject. Concept development and comprehension are thinking processes that can be directed toward knowledge acquisition. Other processes build on these foundations, stressing the application and production of knowledge.

Although knowledge acquisition processes are needed to form the base, that knowledge is useful only to the degree it can be applied or used to create new knowledge. Thus, students need opportunities to use their knowledge, compose, make decisions, solve problems and conduct research to discover or create new knowledge. Through the process of group discussion a number of thinking processes can merge in the student's repertoire of strategies.

Even in the prehistoric hunting and gathering societies, going back over one hundred generations, it was thinking and mutual dependency that made Homoerectus the most sophisticated animal on earth. Critical and creative thinking are natural human processes that can be amplified by awareness and practice. Examples that illustrate core thinking skills are:

1. *Focusing Skills* —attending to selected chunks of information. Some focusing skills include defining, identifying key concepts, recognizing the problem, and setting goals.
2. *Information Gathering Skills* —becoming aware of the substance or content needed. Observing, obtaining information, forming questions, clarifying through inquiry are some skills of information gathering.
3. *Remembering Skills* —are activities that involve information storage and retrieval. Encoding and recalling are thinking skills which have been found to improve retention. These skills involve strategies such as rehearsal, mnemonics, visualization, and retrieval.
4. *Organizing Skills* —arranging information so that it can be understood or presented more effectively. Some of these organizing skills consist of comparing, classifying (categorizing), ordering and representing information.
5. *Analyzing Skills* —are used in classifying and examining information of components and relationships. Analysis is at the heart of critical thinking. Recognizing and articulating attributes and component parts, focusing on details and structure, identifying rela-

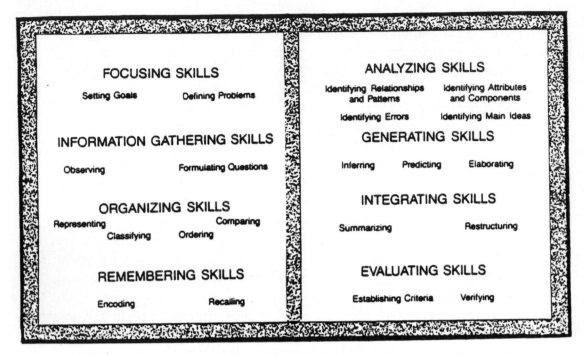

Figure 5.

tionships and patterns, grasping the main idea and finding errors
are elements of analysis.

6. *Generating Skills* —involve using prior knowledge to add information beyond what is known or given. Connecting new ideas, inferring,
   identifying similarities and differences, predicting, and elaborating adds new meaning to information. Generating involves such
   higher-order thinking as making comparisons, constructing metaphors, producing analogies, providing explanations and forming
   mental models.

7. *Integrating Skills* —involve putting things together, solving, understanding, forming principles, and creating composition. These
   thinking strategies involve summarizing, combining information,
   deleting unnecessary material, graphically organizing, outlining,
   and restructuring to incorporate new information.

8. *Evaluating Skills* —assessing the reasonableness and quality of ideas.
   Skills of evaluation include establishing criteria and proving or
   verifying data.[9]

9. Singley, M. & Anderson, J.: *The Transfer of Cognitive Skill.* Cambridge, MA, Harvard University Press, 1989.

Thinking skills appear almost spontaneously, especially among proficient learners. Research has shown that most of these skills can be enhanced by effective instructional conditions and methods.[10] There is strong evidence that many students—especially the younger and lower achievers—need explicit and sustained instruction to become skilled in thinking and monitoring their own thinking processes.

Strategies for Teaching Critical Thinking

It is important to make students aware of the characteristics of critical thinking and provide experiences for its application. True problem solving is one way to become aware of the problem. This involves identifying central questions, posing group strategies for solutions, evaluating alternative possibilities, and developing a plan for implementing the best solution. Discussion and shared decision making are intricately entwined in this process.

Good teachers support diversity, individual learning styles and collaboration. This helps students focus on the thinking process, understand, and step outside the boundaries of experience. This means that the teacher and students open themselves to suggestions, risks, styles of thinking and connections heretofore unexamined.

Some Suggestions for Fostering Critical Thinking:
- Provide opportunities for students to explore different viewpoints.
- Conduct debates and discussions on controversial issues. Students work in groups to present an argument on a topic and present their view to another group. Sides can then be switched and the opposite view defended.
- Role play historical events or current news happenings from conflicting viewpoints. Examine some of the more questionable television news images, whose power is palpable but whose connection to reality is tenuous.
- Watch TV broadcasts that present different viewpoints. (PBS' McNeil Lehr News Hour, for example, frequently interviews individuals with differing perspectives on a problem.)
- Have students write letters to the editor of newspapers, TV or popular journals expressing their stance on an issue of importance.

---

10. Weinstein, C. & Mayer, E.: The teaching of learning strategies. In M.C. Wittrock (Ed.), *Handbook of Research on Teaching.* New York, Macmillan, 1986.

One of the basic goals is to stimulate and encourage a wide range of collaboration and divergent thinking. Children learn these skills—along with social responsibility—from their parents, their environment, and their schools. By discussing important moral dilemmas in history, politics, literature, art, music or sports, students can learn about duty to self and others. The cooperative group process can improve mutual respect for themselves, for thinking, and for learning. Once the doors of deep thinking are opened, the focus can change to group problem solving and even social service.[11]

Suggestions for Confrontation with Multiple-Answer Questions:

- Help students explain and evaluate the knowledge they receive. What is its purpose? What are some examples? What arguments would explain or contradict it?
- Encourage free thinking, not repetition and memorization.
- Provide experiences that go beyond the textbook.
- Have students work in cooperative group settings to solve problems, construct projects, design activities.
- Involve students in decision making—stating goals, generating ideas, devising a plan and carrying it out.
- Teach basic thinking skills: information gathering, organizing, analyzing, summarizing, predicting, inferring, and evaluating.
- Provide a variety of challenging problems which require a collaborative effort.

Beyond specific teaching strategies, an important influence on students' thinking is the climate of the classroom and the behavior that the teacher models. Teachers need to model critical thinking behaviors and set the tone, atmosphere, and setting for learning. Teachers can collaborate with students and with other teachers. Being able to work with others in this way is part of what critical thinking is about. In collaborative problem solving the teacher can help in the clarification of goals and provide stimulating open-ended activities and encourage children—particularly shy children—to interact with each other and share the products of their joint imaginations.

Classrooms organized for active group work create a community of respected individual learners. Such thinking does not thrive in a threatening, intimidating environment where either adult or peer pres-

---

11. Sinnott, J. (Ed.): *Everyday Problem Solving: Theory and Applications.* New York, Praeger, 1989.

sure impedes independence. As De Tocqueville observed in the last century, "When group pressure denigrates the individual the result is a tyranny of the majority." He also suggested that man could be most free in community with others. Peer encouragement and collaboration can widen choice and vision.

Teachers can help by holding groups and individuals accountable. This includes being sensitive to student needs, seeking deeper reasons for collective answers and providing credible sources. In a cooperative teaching environment it is equally important for teachers to be willing to admit mistakes or say "I don't know, how can we find out?"

Opening To the Unfamiliar: Assessing Thinking

The role of teachers is changing along with thinking styles. The old view of teaching as the transmission of content is being expanded to include ways of helping students construct knowledge. The underlying notion is that knowledge is to be shared or developed rather than held by the authority. Teachers, administrators, and parents need to model interpersonal skills and think about thinking themselves.

Students can best come to critically think about—and understand—complex concepts by actively exploring them in cooperative groups.[12] Recognizing the development of critical thinking in action is a good first step toward its application and assessment. Some possible guideposts for assessing development of thinking and collaborative skills include:

- A decrease in "How do I do it?" questions. (Students ask group members before asking the teacher.)
- Using trial-and-error discovery learning without frustration.
- Questioning peers and teachers (asking powerful why questions).
- Using metaphor, simile, allegory, in their speaking, writing, and thinking.
- Developing interpersonal discussion skills for shared inquiry.
- Increased ability to work collaboratively in cooperative groups.
- Willingness to begin a task.
- Initiating inquiry.
- Comfort with ambiguity and open-ended assignments.
- Synthesizing and combining diverse ideas.

---

12. Nicholls, J.: *The Competitive Ethos and Democratic Education.* Cambridge, MA: Harvard University Press, 1989.

It's hard to measure attitudes, thinking and interpersonal skills on a paper-and-pencil test. Another way is to observe the humor, antidotes, parental reactions, and teacher-student interaction. The ability of both students and teachers to pull together as a team influences how well students reflect on their thinking, pose powerful questions, and connect diverse ideas.

> *Relationships to others, like thinking are as incoherent*
> *and difficult to measure as truth. . . .*
> *But when previously unassociated ideas strike together*
> *the result is a little stunning.*

> —Herman Melville

Inventing the Future

As schools try to greet the future, curriculum models must shift to help students critically perceive, analyze, interpret and discover a range of meanings. This isn't easy amidst the glitter of electronic reality. We need educators and students who can learn to ask insightful questions together, self-monitor, reflect on their own thinking, and be able to plan ahead. Part of this planning must include methods for dealing with the unexpected, since no matter how clever the planning, it's impossible to predict many of today's transient situations. The late twentieth century puts such a high tax on the familiar that many future directions in education can't be charted in advance. But having a lesson plan helps.

It seems clear that specialized and general thinking need to interact to maximize the transfer and application of critical thinking skills. When students encourage each other in mastering thinking skills and basic subject matter, new material can be hooked on another group member's existing schemata. Teachers need strategies for teaching critical thinking and for promoting student team learning. Beyond strategies, there is the need for accommodating organizational change in the classroom and in the schools.

This may be the best time to push for a socially interactive curriculum that can develop the thinking skills appropriate for the beginning of a new century. Real change most frequently comes during times when major players in a situation are simultaneously focused on an issue *and* ill at ease. After years of dwelling in a state of suspended animation nearly everyone seems very concerned with what has happened to the

American educational system. But with so many competing social-political issues, the shelf life of pressing educational concerns may be limited.

Cooperative Learning and
Enhancing Cognitive Development

A lot of attention has recently been given to the benefits of cooperative learning. But little attention has been paid to the effect of collaborative problem solving on cognitive development. Over thirty years ago, Piaget suggested that opportunities for becoming less egocentric are much more common when children discuss things with one another. His rationale was that learners must face the reality of different human perspectives (on any given situation) when they take part in active group discussion. Collaboration between peers clearly helps even very young children learn how to take different points of view into account. And when children at different developmental levels work together to explore differences of opinion, they all improve their thinking skills.[13] It seems that coming into verbal contact with peers who use different rules to solve problems predictive powers are improved. And when children jointly try out their hypothesis, results are even more dramatic. The positive effects of such collaboration have proven to go beyond achievement to have a positive effect on cognitive development, self-esteem and the ability to work with others.[14] When children share a goal, the result of trying to reach it can, because of different perspectives, lead to cognitive conflict. Resolving that conflict leads directly to cognitive development.

Catalyst for Change:
Organizing Classrooms for Team Learning

The deep and complex needs of child rearing and education in the late twentieth century cannot be met without the participation of every institution in our society. Schools cannot be expected to provide magical solutions for the nation's international competitiveness. They can, however, serve as a catalyst for collaboration between agencies working on different segments of America's intransigent social and educational ills.

Public attitudes toward child care have rapidly evolved in the 1980s.

---

13. Piaget, J.: *The Moral Judgments of the Child.* New York, The Free Press, 1965.

14. Wertsch, J.: *Culture, Communication and Cognition.* New York, Cambridge University Press, 1985.

Most mothers no longer stay home, and parenting is becoming professionalized. The result is a nation struggling to establish standards for child care in this rapidly growing industry. Child-care providers (among the worst-paid workers in America) need professional standards, teaching techniques, materials, and direction. This is no longer baby-sitting, as it plays a major role in how well the child does later on. Within day-care centers, collaborative problem solving can be a valuable tool for amplifying the cognitive development of young children.

Critical and Creative Thinking

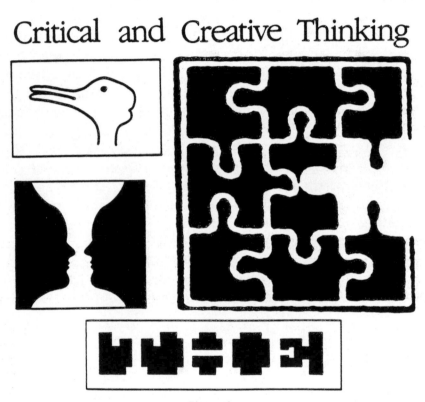

Figure 6.

COLLABORATIVE EDUCATION, SOCIAL RESPONSIBILITY AND COLLECTIVE REASON

It is a profoundly erroneous truism, repeated by all copybooks and by eminent people when they are making speeches, that we should cultivate the habit of always thinking of what we are doing. The precise opposite is the case. Civilization advances by extending the number of operations which we can perform without thinking about them. Operations of thought should be like cavalry charges in battle: strictly limited in number, requiring fresh horses, taking place at decisive moments, and most effective when there is strong mutual support.

—Alfred North Whitehead

American and Western European thinking about the relationship between education and freedom rely primarily on ideas generated during the Enlightenment. Classical liberal philosophers viewed the cultivation of reason, autonomy, and freedom as ways to avoid domination by the collective. The American Revolution grew out of this complex web of democratic yearning, social experimentation, civil entitlement, and deep concern for individual rights. It was the accompanying debate over how to balance individual thinking and group responsibility that fueled the social conditions leading to free public schools.

In this culture civil and educational rights became more directly connected to social, political, cultural, and economic group realities. Tensions between the needs and desires of those who see themselves as upper and lower "middle class" is increasing. This is partly because the wealthy have done better than others. During the last decade the communal forms are constantly changing demanding new community structures. For American democracy to remain on an even keel requires a redesign of our sense of public space and societal membership. This will involve common educational experiences, shared communications, group standards, and a certain level of social cohesion.

Learning to balance the multiple requirements of reason, individualism and community is part of developing a civic consciousness and helping students examine their own socialization process. Interpersonal and intrapersonal skills have never been more important to maintaining a democratic culture. The challenge of civic education is bringing a larger sense of sharing and attachment to a broader societal group. As we enter an extraordinary period of educational transition the central question remains the same: "What forms of thinking and learning can best develop the enabling possibilities of a democratic society?"

Critical thinking and social dialogue cannot be ignored when it comes to educating the untapped possibilities in minds of children. Providing the conditions under which children learn to critically search, exercise their imaginations, and create personal futures is a large part of what education must be about in a democracy. From the mass media to the schools, the quality of public language has traditionally provided a foundation for educating (or miseducating) citizens.

The organizational patterns of institutions *can* make a difference in community dialogue. As far as the schools are concerned, small mixed-ability classroom groups are a useful forum for asking questions, listening to others, summarizing discoveries, and providing group support structures for remaking freedom through choice and action. What must a teacher know to be able to structure reciprocal arrangements for different voices?

The Quality of Public Discourse: Building a Civic Culture

Distinguishing between familiarity and freshness, between cliche and originality, depends as much on social structures as it does on the individual. Good teachers know that students frequently want *answers* when what they need are ideas to grow on. Expanding the possibilities of the human mind requires teachers who can help children achieve freedom in dialogue with others. This means setting up the conditions under which individuals fulfill themselves through self-directed explorations, developing a common core of knowledge, and collaborative public service.

Under a plan sponsored by Senator Kennedy and President Bush a youth service proposal is positioning the schools to play a key role in enabling students to serve society. As part of this effort a National Service Board is being developed to set up school-community partnerships for students and bring volunteers from the community into the schools.

On the national level, the tension between individual authenticity and the press of the material world requires a broad social response to external conditions. In local schools and classrooms collaborative learning structures can help students actively work together to become a community of learners with a social conscience. On an individual level, the mutual support for authenticity can lead to a deeper and more meaningful originality for each student.[15]

The whole process of schooling in America is shaded by the predicament and contradiction. Factors ranging from popular culture to a grow-

---

15. Kagan, J. & Lamb, S. (Eds.): *The Emergence of Morality in Young Children.* Chicago, The University of Chicago Press, 1987.

ing underclass persist in "diseducating" America. As the country moves towards a two-class society, in terms of economic and educational reality, the inequality of prospects is being transmitted from generation to generation. If this continues and the thoughts of a people are diluted by media strip-mining, a hostile home environment, and inferior schooling, both thinking and democratic freedoms will be degraded.[16]

The process of undermining one of the world's most advanced civic cultures obscures extraordinary national possibilities. Vast segments of American culture—from academia to the arts—have faded from public view. Democracy cannot function effectively without the sharing of quality information. If the only information we share is the superficial and ambiguous reality of the electronic media, then the system will not work. Television tells us that everything is fine because the public can get its in-depth information from newspapers. That's not a bad excuse—if only we could get Americans to read. Twenty years ago, two out of three people in their twenties read the newspaper on a regular basis. Now it's down to one out of three. Newspapers may still have a special societal franchise to guard the First Amendment to the Constitution, but the current trend is to mimic television. The *USA Today* newspaper even comes in a TV-shaped box. Is it possible to be viewer or reader friendly without compromising quality?

Education, Thinking Skills and the Global Positioning of Nations

Education is the most prominent area where our nation's shortcoming threaten to impose enormous long-term costs. . . . Rather than being a drain on resources, education makes a useful economic contribution that pays for itself many times over.

—Joint Economic Committee of Congress

As the percentage of citizens of influence who have children in the public schools dropped, America (almost unnoticed) stopped investing in the future. Increasingly, legislators and economists share in recognizing that a reinvigoration of American education is basic to our national survival. Over the last twenty years human resources, technology, and capital equipment were neglected at the very time the world was entering a literacy-intensive era. The question is how to best start and sustain children on the lifelong task of thinking and learning.

---

16. Good, T. & Brophy, J.: *Looking in Classrooms.* New York, Harper & Row, 1987.

Whether we call it the information, learning, or knowledge age, the need for personnel who are technologically competent and functionally literate is without precedent. The need goes beyond the basics. International competition, in an age of continuous change and chaos, requires knowledgeable workers who are good at creative teamwork. The global positioning of countries is depending more and more on the extent to which they have a population with higher level thinking and problem-solving abilities. Increasingly, teachers, students, and everyone else has to take responsibility for different jobs, analyzing alternatives, and handling the freedom needed to search out the touch of new possibilities.[17]

Uncertainty may be the essence of late twentieth century science and art, but teaching cooperative higher level thinking skills is a fundamental (basic) need in the nineties. And with the accent of global business in turbulent and uncertain times there is a premium placed on relationships spanning forms and countries. Corporate collaboration that would have appeared decidedly odd in the eighties is looking more appealing for the 1990s. Even the competitive international firms are beginning to recognize the need for strategic alliances. As borders become less of a barrier, in a rapidly fluctuating world economy, highly developed human potential becomes the key to participation in global markets.

This is not to suggest the public mind must be trained to insure obedient workers for a multinational business world. The concern that many Americans are feeling about education is just as connected to a much broader concern about the country and the planet. Some of the best writers, poets, and scientists would probably not show up for work on time. What's needed—besides a commitment to pay the toll—is a critical aesthetic to inform a diversity of educational styles and support structures. Democratic educational choices lay in the dark domain between highly skilled acquiescence and civic literacy.

Schools as Thoughtful Cooperative Environments

Helping children deal with the paradoxes of late twentieth century America requires dialogue within a community of learners. As students seek a common ground, through speech and action, individual and

---

17. Warshofsky, F.: *The Chip War: The Battle for the World of Tomorrow.* New York, Scribners, 1989.

group preferences for connection can be realized. Both education and the democratic process can be improved by extending collaborative structures that cut across institutional lines.[18] Efforts based on a broad sense of community and social-political coalitions can energize resources and help instill a pattern of lifelong learning. The gradual refinement of the specifics will require careful building cooperative efforts that cut across economic, age, and interest groups.

In the schools, accepting the isolated social reality of past classroom organizational models limits thinking and obstructs creative vision. Approaching new educational reality from a new cooperative direction means more than teaching students to work together in mixed-ability groups. It also involves drawing away from the mesmerizing power of the given and seeing the curriculum and classroom organization with fresh eyes.

Working alone can be lonely and lead to boredom. Peer interaction, when it's done well, can actively engage student energies. Communal dialogue, enriched by a multiplicity of voices, has the potential for stimulating a commitment to critical thinking, learning, and freedom.[19] Support structures vary from subject matter to parents. Content certainly has a role to play in illuminating the excitement, difficulty, and dangers of a democratic education. Responsible adults can model and inculcate values.

How students internalize values is as important as how they act. Assertive discipline may work on a temporary basis, but what is the effect on social responsibility in the future? If actions don't stem from "thoughtful" positions that take place almost unconsciously, a change in circumstances will confuse students and they won't know how to act. Thoughtful school environments should model the behavior that students are to learn.

Assuring real option in the real world calls for greater thoughtfulness in both the thinking and in the social sense. Preparing students who care about others in the immediate small classroom group and in the local community goes hand in hand with good thinking, creative risk-taking and problem solving. Teachers must be key decision makers as we retool the educational system to turn out well-educated and socially responsible young men and women.

There are many educators who are enthusiastic about searching out

---

18. Spring, J.: *Conflicts of Interest — The Politics of American Education.* New York, Longman, Inc., 1988.

19. Green, M.: *The Dialectic of Freedom.* New York, Teachers College Press, 1988.

new cooperative structures and approaches for engendering wonder, civic imagination, and thinking skills for their students. As children actively engage learning in small collaborative groups teachers can be confident that they are making use of basic human nature. Peer interaction reflects the active nature of learning and provides the social support structure necessary for having students test their capacity as performing thinkers—inquiring, solving problems, applying personal knowledge to a new situation. Teachers can rest assured that developing dimensions of cooperation and thoughtfulness in their classrooms not only relates to today's world of work but serves as a vehicle for being free in community, in association with others.

REFERENCES

Adams, D. & Hamm, M.: *Media and Literacy*. Springfield, IL: Charles C Thomas, 1989.

Atwood, M.: *Cat's Eye*. New York: Doubleday, Bantam, Dell Publishing, 1989.

Baron, J. B., & Sternberg, R. J. (Eds.) *Teaching Thinking Skills: Theory and Practice*. New York, Freeman, 1987.

Burns, M.: Teaching "what to do in arithmetic" vs. teaching "what to do and why." *Educational Leadership*, 43, 34–38, 1986.

Connelly, E. M. & Clandinin, D. J.: *Teachers as Curriculum Planners: Narratives of Experience*. New York, Teachers College Press, 1988.

Danto, A.: *Connections To The World*. New York, Harper & Row, 1989.

Dertouzos, M., Lester, R., & Solow, R.: *Made In America*. Cambridge, MA, MIT Press, 1989.

Duckworth, E.: *The Having of Wonderful Ideas and Other Essays on Teaching and Learning*. New York, Teachers College Press, 1987.

Goodlad, J.I.: *A Place Called School*. New York: McGraw-Hill, 1984.

Glick, M. & Holyoak, K.: In Cormier (Ed.), *Transfer of Learning*. NY: Academic Learning Press, 1987.

Good, T. & Brophy, J.: *Looking in Classrooms*. New York, Harper & Row, 1987.

Grant, Wiggins: Creating a thought provoking curriculum. *American Educator*, Winter, 1987.

Greene, M.: *The Dialectic of Freedom*. New York, Teachers College Press, 1988.

Kagan, J. & Lamb, S. (Eds.): *The Emergence of Morality in Young Children*. Chicago, The University of Chicago Press, 1987.

Nicholls, J.: *The Competitive Ethos and Democratic Education*. Cambridge, MA: Harvard University Press, 1989.

Perkins, D. & Solomon, G.: *Thinking: International Conference*. Hillsdale, NJ, Lawrence Erlbaum Associates, 1987.

Research into Practice Digest: *Thinking Skills Series*. Washington, D.C., Center for Research into Practice, 1989.

Resnick, L.: *Education and Learning to Think.* Washington, D.C.: Academy Press, 1987.

Singley, M., & Anderson, J.: *The Transfer of Cognitive Skill.* Cambridge, MA, Harvard University Press, 1989.

Sinnott, J. (Ed.): *Everyday Problem Solving: Theory and Applications.* New York, Praeger, 1989.

Slavin, R. E.: *Cooperative Learning.* New York: Longman, 1983.

Spring, J.: *Conflicts of Interest — The Politics of American Education.* New York, Longman Inc., 1988.

Warshofsky, F.: *The Chip War: The Battle for the World of Tomorrow.* New York, Scribners, 1989.

Weinstein, C. & Mayer, E.: The teaching of learning strategies. In M.C. Wittrock (Ed.), *Handbook of Research on Teaching.* New York, Macmillan, 1986.

Wertsch, J. (Ed.): *Culture, Communication, and Cognition: Vygotskian Perspectives.* New York, Cambridge University Press, 1985.

Wurman, R. S. (1989). *Information Anxiety.* New York: Doubleday.

4

COLLABORATION IN THE LANGUAGE ARTS: CONNECTING READING, WRITING, THINKING AND LEARNING

Teachers—like parents—form our minds, enlarge our visions, and elevate our aspirations. Language, literacy, critical thinking and learning are the very foundations on which cooperation is built in a democratic republic. By emphasizing these concepts good teachers prepare men and women, of all races and circumstances, to exercise the responsibility of citizenship.

—James Freedman[1]

Interest in cooperative learning has grown at the very time some of the routinized and competitive notions about teaching language arts and reading are changing. In a classroom environment where collaboration and thinking are emphasized, the teacher can set the problem and organize students into small groups so that they can collaborate in working it out. This kind of active multi-ability group work and peer tutoring has proved to be a useful vehicle for gaining social insights, enhancing thinking skills, and learning basic subject matter.[2] Programs to incorporate thinking and interpersonal skills into the language arts curriculum are being developed throughout the country.

Literacy is a social process that grows best when small groups work together to discuss and reflect on what they are writing and reading.[3] Social interaction can help individuals extract meaning from text, especially when small groups share together in a caring manner. Fostering dialogue and mutual consensus about problems in the world outside of school is also important, since real-world problems tend to be less well structured than those found in the best curriculum. Additionally, the

---

1. Freedman, James, O.: Commencement Address, Dartmouth College, 1989.

2. Bruffee, K. A.: "Collaborative Learning and the Conversation of Mankind," *College English,* Vol. 46., 1984.

3. Vygotsky, L. *Thought and Language.* Cambridge, MA, MIT Press, 1986.

group process and critical thinking skills brought to bear on such problems will better prepare students for adulthood.[4]

Pairing students is the easiest way to introduce them to the mixed-ability group experience. They can be randomly assigned, pupils can choose or students can write down four people they would like to work with, and the teacher chooses from the list. Larger groups can be formed from these two-person teams to analyze, synthesize, and evaluate language activities.

When learning tasks are assigned it is helpful if the students know what aspects of the work are for individuals, pairs and small groups. It is also up to the teacher to point out the goals of a lesson, placing students in groups and making sure that the right materials are available. The teacher encourages group work, monitors progress, and assesses student performance. Collaboration in language arts instruction makes positive use of mixed-ability grouping as diverse groups of students share a wide range of perspectives. After they have shared information and helped each other learn, the entire team's performance can be evaluated.

Effective Group Communications in Language Arts Instruction

Writers in the world outside of school often collaborate to help the act of writing, insight, and feeling come together more powerfully. To further students' understanding this point, teachers can encourage them to randomly examine a library shelf, magazine, or scholarly journal to spot how many works are jointly authored. In group discussions of coauthored stories—or writing together—students must know when to assume different roles, like researcher, summarizer, animator (activator), or recorder. Some teachers even like to assign different group roles so that students can experience and develop the strategies for dealing with isolated, overly talkative, or non-task-oriented group members. This allows them to practice strategies of good listening, clarifying, or disagreeing in a non-threatening manner. Groups can even be stopped from time to time while a randomly selected student summarizes what has been said—or individuals write down what they have heard. Perceptions can then be compared.[5]

---

4. Sternberg, R. J.: Teaching critical thinking: Are we making critical mistakes?" *Phi Delta Kappan, 67,* 1985.

5. Hansen, J.: *When Writers Read.* Portsmouth, NH, Heinemann, 1987.

In the last few years teachers have been trying to move from basal readers to reading real books—literature. This whole language approach has proven to have a positive effect on reading ability—as well as a profound effect on children's writing. If children read good writing it has a positive effect on their own writing.[6] In a student-centered language arts/reading curriculum, students can collaboratively cross-teach techniques. Active group activities, built on positive interdependence, hold each individual or pair responsible for contributing to the achievement of a common goal.

In "whole language" literacy circles, students can be helped by the process of communicating with peers' writers (real readers) who can provide immediate feedback during the writing or revision process. Children need to develop the skill to go beyond "the introduction is good" to "how do you fulfill the expectations your introduction set up?" Such student-centered, higher-level group questions are also an essential part of the cooperative group writing process.[7] Having children share a brief passage with their group can also heighten interest in what other group members may want to read in the future.

In collaborative frameworks for language arts instruction students are encouraged to discuss the work they are doing on writing projects, problems they are solving or books that they are reading. Teachers can vary the way this is done. At times the issues they read or write about can be a topic for group discussion; at other times students can help structure the framework for discussion, evaluating evidence, making predictions, or developing a line of thought. And by moving activities built on collaboration and higher order thinking skills into the center of the curriculum, students can assimilate concepts through peer interaction.[8]

The national report, *Becoming a Nation of Readers*, points out that children spend only about 6 percent of their time in the classroom actually reading. Paradoxically, the research suggests that the more time they spend reading, the better they do on reading achievement tests.[9] There is no question about actually reading books—or having the teacher read to them—having a positive effect on the reading process.

6. Burns, P., Roe, B., & Ross, E.: *Teaching Reading in Today's Elementary Schools.* Boston, Houghton Mifflin, 1988.

7. Salmon, P., and Claire, H.: *Classroom Collaboration.* London, Rutledge & Kagan, 1984.

8. Resnick, L.: *Education and Learning to Think.* Report. Washington, D.C., National Academy Press, 1987.

9. Conley, M.: "Grouping." *Research Within Reach.* Newark, DE, International Reading Association, 1987.

Background on Literature-Based Instruction

The current research and theory in the learning and teaching of language arts supports the use of literature for the development of student literacy.[10] Further, research and theory favor the use of whole, meaningful works rather than excerpts or revisions.[11] Nevertheless, many reading programs in elementary schools still depend on basal reading systems that focus on discrete skills and the use of contrived stories that have a controlled vocabulary. Educators are currently struggling to bring practice in literacy instruction into harmony with current knowledge by shifting from basal reading systems to literature-based approaches. Some school districts devote two days a week to the basal reading series; others have thrown them out altogether. Textbook publishers fearing that the market is drying up have even developed "literature-based" basals.

Whatever the arrangement, whole language instruction provides a promising collaborative framework for focusing on meaning and the communicative process. The quality of intrinsic, critical thinking and peer support depends on the time allowed for reflection, group experimentation and holistic language processing. When the emphasis is on indirect, child-centered instruction, the teacher sets the framework and students use good literature, their own writing, and authentic oral language. In the whole language approach teachers treat students like they are members of the same literacy club, rather than textbound pupils searching for "correct answers."[12]

Directed Reading and Thinking

Reading is much more than extracting facts; it involves the making of meaning (from the printed word) and connecting with a rich literacy tradition. Students do not have to read the same book in order to discuss a book's attributes with others. Developing critically thinking readers means teaching students to anticipate story outcomes, discuss high level questions, infer meaning, and extrapolate to other situations.

In a directed reading thinking activity (DRTA) students try to predict

---

10. National Council of Teachers of English, 1988.

11. International Reading Association, 1987.

12. Smith, F.: *Reading Without Nonsense.* New York: Teachers College Press, 1985.

Figure 7.

ahead on the basis of a few clues that they have been given. As they read they continue to jointly speculate about the story and hypothesize. Divergent responses are encouraged—although opinions must be justified on some logical basis. After the story, students demonstrate their understanding by using rather than simply recalling important points. In the early grades predictable books, like *Curious George*, can teach the same thinking and prediction skills.

Collaborative DRTA activities can be a positive influence as we move from the traditional emphasis on reading skills to a collaborative literature approach emphasizing critical thinking skills. Critical thinking abilities relate to making inferences about daily and special events. These skills might be thought of as "reasonable reflective thinking that is focused on deciding what to believe or do."[13] When mixed-ability reading and writing groups are used in combination, directed writing and thinking activities (DWTA) can serve as a vehicle for allowing ideas to come to fruition and for helping others decide where to go with their stories. Literature serves as a resource for seeing how adult writers go about setting the scene for more elaborate presentation of ideas. The research suggests that collaboratively reading and writing together prompts

---

13. Ennis, R.: "A Taxonomy of Critical Thinking Dispositions and Abilities." In *Teaching Thinking Skills: Theory and Practice.* J. Boyokoff Baron & R. Sternberg, (Eds.). New York, W.H. Freeman & Co., 1987.

more critical thinking and imaginative storytelling.[14] Directly connecting reading and writing programs also proved effective in achieving multiple perspectives and a greater depth of understanding.[15]

Reading activities can include having partners read to each other, making predictions based on visual (or written) clues, or jointly constructing summaries after reading the story. Peer conferences can occur during the planning, revision and editing process. Cooperative groups of four to six help students learn to listen, question, resolve conflicts, share resources, and make decisions. In cooperative groups much of the responsibility for learning is placed where it belongs: on the students.

Critical Thinking and Improving Reading Comprehension

Inductive Reasoning Grid

Name of character _____

Reading Clues: *Interpretation:*

1. Statements by the character:

_____   _____
_____   _____

2. Character's actions:

_____   _____
_____   _____

3. Character's thinking patterns:

_____   _____
_____   _____

4. What others say about this character:

_____   _____
_____   _____

5. Situations the character becomes involved in:

_____   _____
_____   _____

6. Other important information about the character:

_____   _____
_____   _____

Summary of the character: *My generalizations about the character:*

14. Marcel, A. & Carpenter, P.: *The Psychology of Reading and Language Comprehension.* Newton, MA, Allen and Bacon, 1987.

15. R. Tierney, A. Soter, J. O'Flahavan, & W. McGinley: "The Effects of Reading and Writing Upon Thinking Critically," *Reading Research Quarterly.* 24(2), 1989.

Seeking Visions: Writing as a Cooperative Learning Process

Good writing has more to do with reading good literature and writing a lot than it does with any collection of rules. Improving communication and social skills is a goal that can be reached through critical thinking, innovative thought, concern for the audience, and the realization that the group swims or sinks together. It's important to for the students to encourage each other to read more fully and critically so that they can write less simplistically.[16]

The ideas that follow are offered as suggestions to promote thinking collaboratively and critically about the writing process.

1. Sharing Quotes in the prewriting process:

Share a quote at your students' level and ask them to respond to it.

"Writing, like life itself, is a voyage of discovery." — Henry Miller

"Poems are like dreams, you put into them what you don't know you know." — A. Rich

"Writing and rewriting are a constant search for what one is saying." — J. Updike

"A writer keeps surprising himself . . . he doesn't know what he is saying until he sees it on the page." — T. Williams

"One of the reasons a writer writes, I think, is that his stories reveal so much he never thought he knew." — C. Holland

"The relationship of talk to writing is central to the writing process." — J. Britton

"Writing a play is thinking, not thinking about thinking." — R. Bolt

"Writing has got to be an act of discovery . . . I write to find out what I'm thinking about." — E. Albee

"How do I know what I think until I see what I say?" — E. M. Forester

2. Using Quotes in Collaborative Writing

Try focusing on ways to use embed quotes in personal responses — or quote to support visual imagery.

"Experimenting in composing with words is experimenting in composing understanding, in composing knowledge. A writer, in a sense, composes the world in which he or she lives. — K. Dowst

"An essential part of the writing process is explaining the matter to oneself." — J. Britton

---

16. Perfetti, C.: *Reading Ability.* New York, Oxford University Press, 1985.

"During the class the students should not be passive receivers of information. They must be doers, writing and rewriting discovering what they have to say, discovering what they need to know to say it effectively — until the students complete the act of writing by reaching a reader who understands what they have written." — D. Murray

"Writing usually begins in the self and the composing process is, in part, a search for appropriate modes of approach to an audience. The writer relates his work to his own experience; he must develop this thought on the basis of what he knows." — B. Peterson

"Far from doing away with paper the computer has made all trees in their vicinity quake in terror." — D. Adams

If students connect their personal lives to events in literature, writing and literature can be a window on the world — or on oneself. Quality literature and writing can be approached with a sense of discovery. Having peers and the teacher give feedback to students is a key to improving cooperative behavior. For students, one of the most frequently mentioned cooperative group pleasures is sharing different points of view and combining group ideas.[17]

COLLABORATION AND WRITING

Groups of between four and six student can generate ideas by brainstorming, discussing issues in the news, or sharing a book they have read during the prewriting process. Listening to new ideas can help pairs of students draft possibilities that can contribute to the overall group writing project. After the material has been developed by individuals or pairs it can be brought together for revision. Here, students can exchange drafts and solve overall writing problems by focusing on specific elements.

By turning their language arts classrooms into collaborative ventures, teachers find that students are more willing to select their own topics and explore subjects of real interest to them.[18] Drawing on ideas from class, their personal lives, and reading serves as a powerful catalyst for thinking, learning, and developing the art of writing.

---

17. Hall, M. A.: *Teaching Reading as a Language Experience.* Columbus, OH, Merrill, 1981.

18. Gere, A. R. (Ed.): *Roots in the Sawdust: Writing to Learn Across the Disciplines.* Urbana, IL, National Council of Teachers of English, 1985.

Peer Editing

Peer editing requires comprehension, reasoning and reflection. To be an effective evaluator, student editors should come to a piece of writing with specific questions in mind. The questions on the following checklist can be applied to any kind of writing.

1. What is the focus or main idea of the draft?
2. Are the supporting details related directly to this focus?
3. What additional details should the writer add?
4. Does the draft have a clear organization?
5. Is there anything I find confusing?
6. Are there any awkward or unclear sentences or paragraphs?
7. What do I think or feel after reading the draft? Are these the effects the writer intended?
8. What do I like best about the draft?

Peer editors should keep these points in mind:

- Be sensitive to the writer's feelings and needs. Be courteous.
- Point out strengths as well as weaknesses.
- Supply constructive criticism. Offer suggestions for improvement.
- Focus on ideas and form rather than proofreading.

Most of the editing can be left to the students—sentence structure, paragraphing or which paper is to go first, second or third in the final group product. This has proven a better learning process than simply having the teacher collect the first draft and suggest revisions.[19]

To learn to write, children need to know adults who write. So, modeling behavior on the part of the teacher is important.[20] Besides working with their peers, students need to see the teacher in the process of composing. And they needed to see the messy drafts as the teacher moves toward the final product. What can make writing exciting and challenging instead of upsetting, overwhelming, angering, or boring?

---

19. Irwin, J. (Ed.): *Understanding and Teaching Cohesion Comprehension.* Newark, DE, International Reading Association, 1986.

20. Ozick, C.: *Metaphor & Memory.* New York, Knopf, 1989.

COLLABORATIVE WRITING

This section is about students' collaborative struggle in learning to write, read and search for literacy. It is also about the bad aspects of peer relationships and measures that can be taken to enhance the positive and soften negative peer relations. The information in this section is part of a five-year study by Linda Miller Cleary, which explored the interaction of emotion and thought in writing by investigating the experience and context of writing students.

Miller Cleary's data has come from multiple and convergent methodologies: phenomenological in-depth interviews, classroom observations, and composing aloud sessions. She observed a wide range of ability groups, ethnic populations, and social classes.

The Presence of Peers[20a]

In the elementary school, *peers matter*, particularly for students whose families deviate from the middle-class norm. By the adolescent years, peers matter even more. The following is a brief glimpse of what a typical writer, "Lisa," thinks about while writing a "Gothic" short story.

> He beckoned her in . . . his frantic beckoning . . . no his frantic calls to her made her run up the . . . made her run . . . frantic . . . calls . . . made . . . her run up the. . . . What? . . . the sidewalk . . . n they're rich . . . stone . . . path . . . yes, the stone path to her house . . . and she . . . When she arrived at the door . . . Amin . . . Aminadab . . . was blocking her view to the inside . . . No . . . Mrs. Arkus, you may not go in there, you mustn't . . . That's stupid . . . (disgust in voice) . . . I . . . I can't think of what to say . . . stupid paper . . . Oh God! I don't really like anything I've written . . .

Three things are apparent from this small section: (1) that standard writer Lisa is automatic at transcription; (2) that she can think, plan, and write simultaneously; and (3) that she has an inner critic at work when she writes, an internalized representation of past critical audiences ready and waiting in her conscious attention to pounce on any slip of the mind or pen.

Audience factors affect Lisa's relationship with her material. The extent to which an audience will affect the writer is a function of the self-

---

20a. Cleary, Linda Miller: "Lisa: The Powerful Presence of Peers." *Student Struggle for Voice.* In Press Portsmouth, N.H.: Boynton/Cook of Heinemann Education Books.

concept and a function of the development of a writer's transcription abilities. Very young writers' sense of self is egocentric. Donald Graves describes the gift of self-centered confidence the beginning writer has:

> The child will make no greater progress in his entire school career than in the first year of school simply because self centeredness makes him fearless. The world must bend to his will. This child screens out audience. . . . The child centers on a very narrow band of thinking and ignores other problems in the field.[21]

As writing becomes more automatic, children become more aware of audience and take it into consideration during writing. As children grow to adolescence, the way they feel about themselves begins to be largely reflected from peers instead of significant adults. If peers are actively present in the writing environment, writing will assuredly become a relationship between the writer, the material, and that peer audience.

Responding to Others

To a large extent, the view that developing writers come to have of themselves as students and writers is reflected from the response they get to their work. Elementary school children attend carefully to how teachers react to them, and they compare their progress with those around them. They can count stars and smiley faces or the absence of them. Rarely are children oblivious to their reading group level, and they often take measure of themselves on that basis.

Teachers assist in comparison by giving formal and numerical renderings of comparison and by setting up the reading group levelings which so upset many students. In Cleary's study, grades and group status were destructive criteria by which students compared themselves to others.[22]

Language was another medium by which students compared themselves. Whereas basic students were relatively unaware that language was a problem for them, both standard and advanced writers continually compared their use of language with that of other students in the writing classroom.

Comparison with peers affected the way students viewed themselves as readers and writers, but reflected response to their performance also formed their view of themselves. Many adolescent writers remembered

---

21. Graves, D.: *Writing. Teachers and Children at Work.* Exeter, NH, Heinemann, 1983, p. 239.

22. Cushenbery, D.: *Comprehensive Reading Strategies for All Secondary Students.* Springfield, IL, Charles C Thomas, 1988.

being humiliated in their very early reading or writing, and these responses caused later struggle in writing. One student, David, described his early reading experience:

> Even though I am great at math, in first grade I was really slow in reading. We'd go around in the group and read out loud. It was awful. I can read alone fine now, but when I read in front of class, I still fumble, get really nervous, and I start to sweat. I had a lot of frustration with writing in first grade too 'cause I was slow. All the other kids would get their assignments done, and I used to never get my work done. One day I finished my work, and that time the whole class stood up and clapped. It was like they were making fun of me. The principal came in and said, "What's going on here?" The teacher said, "Well, David finally finished his work for the day, so we're showing him our appreciation."

Even in the elementary schools, round-robin reading is debilitating for everyone. Good readers have their rates slowed, particularly if they have to listen to someone read poorly. And the poor reader is humiliated.[23]

Adolescents go to even greater lengths to avoid negative responses from peers. Erik Erikson noted that an adolescent would rather act "shamelessly in the eyes of his elders, out of free choice, than be forced into activities which would be shameful in his own eyes or in those of his peers." Many students will go to extremes to protect themselves from a public display of incompetence.

Adolescents begin to see themselves in the reflected light of peer responses. This peer mirror makes them vulnerable, even desperate at times. Lisa defended herself from public criticism by refusing to engage in writing, by playing truant, by saying she didn't care, even by risking one humiliation (risking a confusing reading) to avoid another (admitting that she had written about whales). By the time the participants were in junior high, even the best of students feared exposure that might make them look foolish in front of their peers. A student's openness to support or advice was related to her past experience with writing, to her confidence in the piece to be reviewed, to the size of the group, and, most importantly, to the trust she felt in its members.

To maximize trust, permit students some say in the way they are grouped and in the audiences to which their work is exposed. Many teachers permit students to select groups using preset criteria. Some

---

23. Hladczuck, J., & Elter, W.: *Comparative Reading: An International Bibliography.* Westport, CT, Greenwood Press, 1987.

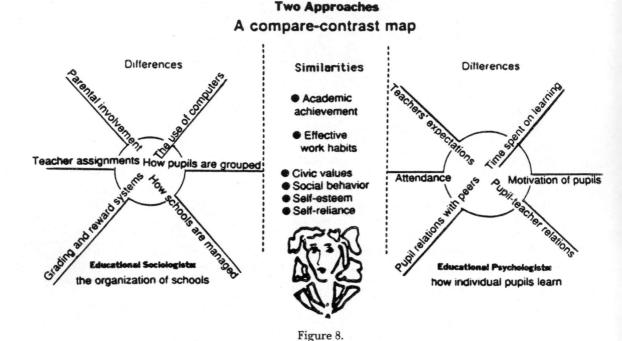

Two Approaches
A compare-contrast map

Differences

Parental involvement

The use of computers

Teacher assignments   How pupils are grouped

Grading and reward systems   How schools are managed

Educational Sociologists:
the organization of schools

Similarities

● Academic
  achievement

● Effective
  work habits

● Civic values
● Social behavior
● Self-esteem
● Self-reliance

Differences

Teachers' expectations   Time spent on learning

Attendance   Motivation of pupils

Pupil relations with peers   Pupil-teacher relations

Educational Psychologists:
how individual pupils learn

Figure 8.

teachers simply say, "Form your own groups of three, making sure that there is a male and a female in each group." Neil Witikko, a Minnesota teacher, forms ongoing groups by having students turn in confidential group preference lists. Each student writes down three peers with whom they would like to work and, if necessary, the name of one person with whom it would be difficult to work. Trying to accommodate their requests, he keeps groups small (3 or, if necessary, 4) to permit a diversity of opinion at the same time as making trust more possible. If a problem group surfaces, he works with the group to raise trust or changes membership to solve the problem.

When structured peer involvement in writing was voluntary and comfortable, the impact on the writing was remarkable. But when the writer didn't trust the peer audience, even the anticipation of that peer exposure could cause the student to struggle. Writers also needed their own topics, regular chunks of time, and good models (literature) to read.

In working out ways to accommodate coauthors' needs—for discussion and for separation from other groups—it was necessary to arrange the classroom as a workshop-like space with quiet isolated corners where students could discuss their work. Students also liked having a workshop materials center, containing everything a writer might need, and a space where they could work with a partner. Some of the most gleeful writing that occurred for peer audiences was the contraband note writing. Every student in the study reported that they had done it. Note writing was peer inspired, voice laden, and meaning driven. It provided practice and permitted students to become more automatic at transcription so that they had more room in the conscious attention for more complex tasks. It was free of constraint and was never reported to be troublesome to the participant. This kind of writing was a mutual getting-on in adolescence that teachers couldn't have prevented if they wanted to.

Additional informal peer help with school writing also went on outside of the classroom in the halls, lunchrooms, and study halls. Kathy said:

> We'd say, "Let me see your's." It made me work harder. We could look over each other's thesis and major supports. I could see her's were a lot better than mine, so I worked on mine.

Doug said:

> My friend asked me to proofread her essay in study hall. She had all these bland spaces that she had filled in with big words from the Thesaurus. They had a different meaning than she was trying to say. I said, "Not so flowery; just say what you want to say." This was intense for me. I was giving somebody advice on writing! The only thing I had learned about writing, and I could tell her.

And most important, peer-inspired writing went on outside of the school building . . . at least through junior high.

Writing Outside of School

Writing for specific purposes did continue for some students outside of school, and most of it was inspired by peers. Letter writing abounded when students had out-of-town romances and friendships that ran concurrent with low budgets. Every female participant and some males wrote in journals at some point during their adolescence, though few still did so by the time they got to high school. Emotional upheaval in students' lives also engendered writing for the more successful students. Elizabeth was most conscious of its benefits:

> It is an outlet. It helps me to collect my thoughts. When you write it all down, you can look at it. I guess it helps me analyze what I'm feeling.

You realize that things are not so big that they're going to take over your life — that you're going to get through them.

Unlike assigned writing where concentration was sometimes interrupted by peer and family problems, this cathartic writing allowed the writer to make sense of the upheaval in their world. Problems did not disrupt conscious attention; they were the focus of conscious attention, and several students mentioned that, if troubled, they often did this kind of writing just so they could get on with their homework. Several males and many females talked about unsent letters that they wrote to rehearse what they wanted to say or to write what they couldn't say.

Peer involvement in the writing classroom is one of the ways that we can return creativity into the classroom. This involvement must be structured carefully. If students are placed in "ability" groups in the early grades, then heterogeneous cooperative groups will be more difficult to form later. Students need to feel comfortable with their peer audience. If they don't, the student will lose an important source of motivation for writing.[24] Supporting each other in observation, critical thi king skills, and the art of writing can help lead to literacy in the fullest sense. Designing writing curricula so that students are writing for peer audiences that they trust, utilizing the workshop model, and designing writing tasks so that peers can work collaboratively towards a common goal fosters intrinsic motivation in writing at all levels.

ASSESSMENT

Processing and Thinking About
Written Expression in Association with Others

It's important to emphasize the need for a *community* of writers because it is a powerful way to help *individuals* develop.[25] Whether writing is self-, peer-, or teacher-evaluated, it is important not to lose sight of the connection between what is valued and what is valuable. Jointly developed folders (portfolios) have a major role to play in student writing assessment by providing a running record of what a child can and can't do.

---

24. Davidson, J., & Koppenhaver, D.: *Adolescent Literacy: What Works Best and Why.* New York, Garland Publishing, 1989.

25. Heilbrun, C.: *Writing A Woman's Life.* New York, Norton, 1989.

The selection that follows offers criteria and descriptions for another type of assessment.

To work toward less control teachers need to help students take more responsibility for their own learning. The ability to evaluate does not come easily at first, and peer writing groups will need teacher-developed strategies to help them process what they have learned. The ability to reflect on being a member of a peer writing team is a form of metacognition—learning to think about thinking and changing behavior as a result. This requires processing in a circular or U-shaped group where all students can see each other. Questions for evaluative processing might include:

- How did group leadership evolve?
- Was it easy to get started?
- How did you feel if one of your ideas was left out?
- What did you do if most members of your group thought that you should write something differently?
- How did you rewrite?
- Did your paper say what you wanted it to?
- What kind of a setting do you like for writing?
- How can you arrange yourself in the classroom to make the writing process better?
- What writing tools did you use?
- How do you feel when you write?

Holistic Grading of Written Expression

This process is now a major way to grade written experiences—from the elementary school through college. It involves looking at how the overall concepts are developed instead of concentrating on mechanical errors.[26] This can be used with a student's writing portfolio. When students learn to maintain portfolios of their work, they can learn to assess their progress and the progress of peers. Writing portfolios can include holistic scores of peers and teachers on writing samples, and work samples of final drafts of the writing process. When this is done, students, teachers, and parents can look over a student's writing history and help widen the range and fluidity.

---

26. Stotsky, S.: *Holistic Scoring of School-Based Writing.* ERIC #196011.

Criteria for Holistic Scoring

Grades 5/6   Clearly above average papers that demonstrate strength in virtually all the criteria. Rarely are these flawless papers, but they are usually substantial in content and often original in idea and/or expression. A "5" tends to be thinner or weaker in some ways than a clearly "6" superior. For example, if third graders are asked to write about how to build a swing, you could actually do it from this paper.

Grades 3/4   Papers ranging from slightly below average ("3") to slightly above average ("4"), either combining strengths with weaknesses in the various criteria or showing an overall sense of underdevelopment. (The swing might get built if you read this paper.)

Grade 1/2   Clearly below average papers which fail to demonstrate competence on several of the criteria (often because the paper is too short) or which are generally empty or which fail to respond to the question. A "2" tends to have redeeming qualities absent in a "1." (There is little chance that someone could build anything from this one.)

Grade 0   Papers which are *wholly* off topic. Such papers neither state nor imply that a change of any kind has taken place. (It's about paper airplanes, rather than swing building.)

Sample Writing Stimulus

If you think about it, you're really not the same person you were four or five years ago. Your ideas, tastes, attitudes, and perhaps even your goals have changed—probably in several ways. Choose any one person (a relative, a teacher, a friend, or anyone else) or any event or experience (a course, a trip, a conversation, or any other event or experience) that has made a difference in your life, and explain as fully as you can how the person or event has changed you. Be as specific as you can in showing how you are different now because of the person or event. In writing your composition be aware of the following elements:

- *ideas* —The extent to which the thoughts and content of the essay are original, insightful, and clear
- *supporting* —The extent to which the ideas of the essay are supported

by examples and details which are specific, appropriate, original, and well developed.

- *unity* — The extent to which the parts of the essay are connected to each other and all help achieve the goal of the essay.
- *style* — The extent to which the language of the essay is used creatively and correctly and helps achieve the writer's goals.

In most informed assessment of writing pupils are asked to produce a written sample. Then the student's peers or teacher looks at:

1. *fluency* — A measure that involves factors such as length of sentences. In general, the longer the sentences tend to be, the higher the fluency.
2. *sentence types* — Are they fragmented? The goal is to combine sentence fragments and vary the type.
3. *vocabulary* — Are the words limited or does the student make good use of unusual words in a passage?
4. *structure, sequence and grammar* — important in the final product.
5. *ideas* — Are they interesting, original, and to the point?

EFFECTIVE GROUP COMMUNICATION— SOME "BASICS" OF POETRY

Poetry is not just "bad prose." To read or write it involves awareness of certain elements that make it unique. Teachers must have some basic knowledge of the vocabulary of poetry in order to help children enjoy and mature in their understanding and appreciation of it. Some characteristics include:

1. Poetry uses condensed language; every word is important.
2. Poetry uses figurative language (e.g. metaphor, simile, personification, irony)
3. The language of poetry is rhythmical (regular, irregular, metered).
4. Some words may be rhymed (internal, end of line, runover) or non-rhyming.
5. Poetry uses the language of sounds (alliteration, assonance, repetition).
6. The units of organization are line arrangements in stanzas or idea arrangements in story, balance, contrast, buildup, surprise, and others.

7. Poetry uses the language of imagery (sense perceptions reproduced in the mind).[27]

Types of Poetry

1. Fixed Forms

a. Narrative or storytelling
b. Literary forms with prescribed structures (e.g., limerick, ballad, sonnet, haiku, others)
c. Lyric

2. Free Verse

a. Tone: humorous, serious, nonsensical, sentimental, dramatic, didactic
b. Content: humor, nonsense, everyday things, animals, seasons, family, fantasy, people, feelings, adventure, moods
c. Time of Writing: contemporary, traditional[28]

3. An Example of Collaborative Poetry

Students work in small collaborative groups. Each team is given a short time (one or two minutes) to compose the first line of a poem. On a signal from the teacher, each team passes their paper to the next group and receives one from another. The group reads the line that the preceding team has written and adds a second line. The signal is given and the papers rotate again—each time the group reads and adds another line. Teams are encouraged to write what comes to mind, even if it's only their name. They must write something in the time allotted. After 8 or 10 lines the papers are returned to their original team. Groups can add a line if they choose, revise and edit the poem they started. The poems can then be read orally, with team members alternating reading the lines. Later, some of them can be turned into an optic poem (creating a picture with computer graphics using the words of the poem) or acted out using ribbons or penlights (while someone else reads the poem).

---

27. Denman, G.: *When You've Made It Your Own...; Teaching Poetry to Young People.* Portsmouth, N.H. Heinemann Educational Books, 1989.

28. Easthope, A.: *Poetry and Phantasy.* Cambridge, Cambridge University Press, 1988.

Poetry to be shared

Some children prefer poems that are humorous with clear-cut rhyme and rhythm. The narrative is the most popular poetic form and favorite topics are familiar experiences and animals. The following poets write poetry whose content and form reflect the modern world. Some write primarily for younger or older children, others for both.[29]

Arnold Adoff	Dorothy Aldis
Byrd Baylor	Harry Behn
Bodecker, N.M.	Gwendolyn Brooks
John Ciardi	Aileen Fisher
Eleanor Farjeon	Elizabeth Coatsworth
Beatrice de Regniers	Zhenya Gay
Eloise Greenfield	Nikki Giovanni
Mary Ann Hoberman	X.J. Kennedy
Patricia Hubbell	Langston Hughes
Karla Kuskin	David McCord
Marci Ridlin Livingston	Myra Cohn Lilian Moore
Ogden Nash	Richard Hughes
Lillian Morrison	Jack Prelutsky
Mary O'Neil	Kay Starbird
Shel Silverstein	Wm. J. Smith
Zilpha Snyder	James Trippett
Judith Viorst	

Anthologies of contemporary poems by a variety of poets:

Stephen Dunning	Lee Bennett Hopkins
Nancy Larrick	Richard Lewis

Structured and Unstructured Poetry Experiences

1. Poetry with Movement and Music

Poems can be put to music and movement. Students can also illustrate picture books or poems to share with younger children.

---

29. Hollander, J.: *Melodious Guile: Fictive Pattern in Poetic Language.* New Haven, CT, Yale University Press, 1989.

2. Daily Oral Reading of Poetry

Students sign up and read aloud at the end of each day. Other students "point," commenting on parts of the poem that catch their attention. A classroom anthology of poetry can be illustrated and laminated.

3. Responding During Free Writing Period

Thirty minutes to an hour and one half is set aside each day for students to write on any topic, in whatever form they choose. A share time follows so that other students may respond to each other's writing by pointing and asking questions.

4. Literature Share Time

Students gather in small groups once a week to share books they have been reading. The groups are structured so that each student

1) reads the author and title of each book
2) tells about the book
3) reads one or two pages aloud
4) receives responses from members of the group, specifically pointing out parts they liked and asking questions.[30]

5. Wish Poems

Each student writes a wish on a strip of paper. The wishes are read together as a whole for the group. Students then write individual wish poems which are shared.

6. Group Metaphor Comparisons

Poems containing metaphors are read aloud. Group comparison poems are written on the board. Students write individual comparison poems and share them with the class.

7. Sample Poetry Lesson

A lesson developed from *Dinosaurs*, a poetry anthology for children edited by Lee Bennett Hopkins.

1. Teacher reads poems aloud.
2. Students brainstorm reasons why the dinosaurs died and words that relate to how the dinosaurs moved.

---

30. Nell, V.: *Lost in a Book.* New Haven, CT, Yale University Press, 1989.

3. Models of dinosaurs and pictures are displayed and talked about.
4. Students write poems and share them.

CREATIVE DRAMA AND GROUP COLLABORATION

Creative drama can be used to bridge the gap between written and visual forms of communication. For example, students can work in small groups to script, act and even videotape a one-minute commercial. They can then critically examine the reasoning behind each group's presentation to the class. Activities can be as simple as picking a topic, deciding how the group will present it...practice the skit and perform it for the class.

Features of Creative Drama

Creative drama has many facets and applications. Performance is not emphasized.

Creative drama:

- Adapts to many types of lessons and subjects (English, Social Studies, Health, Creative Writing, Science, etc.).
- Encourages the clarification of values.
- Evokes contributions and responses from students who rarely participate in "standard" discussions.
- Evaluates, in English classes, how well students know the material (characterization, setting, plot, conflicts).
- Provides a stimulating prewriting exercise.

Creative dramatics emphasizes four fundamental educational objectives:

1. provides for self-realization in unified learning experiences
2. offers firsthand experiences in democratic behavior
3. provides functional learning which is related to life
4. contributes to comprehensive learning

Teaching Story Dramatization

1. Select a good story—and then tell it to the group.
2. With the class, break the plot down into sequences, or scenes, that can be acted out.
3. Have groups select a scene they wish to dramatize.

4. Instruct the groups to break the scene or scenes into further sequence, and discuss the setting, motivation, characterizations, roles, props, etc. Encourage students to get involved in the developmental images of the characters—what they did, how they did it, why they did it. Have groups make notes on their discussions.
5. Meet with groups to review and discuss their perceptions. Let them go into conference and plan in more detail for their dramatization.
6. Have the whole class meet back together and watch the productions of each group. Instruct students to write down five things they liked and five things that could be improved in the next playing.
7. Let the players return to their groups at the end of all group performances and evaluate the dramas using the criteria in number 6.
8. Allow groups to bring back their group evaluations to the whole class. Discuss findings, suggestions, and positive group efforts.

Reminders and Pointers

1. Do not rush students. Side coach if necessary. Examples: "Take your time." "You're doing fine."
2. Try to keep an environment where each can find his own nature without imposition. Growth is natural to everyone.
3. A group of individuals who act, agree, and share together create strength and release knowledge surpassing the contribution of any single member.
4. If during sessions students become restless and static in their work, it is a danger sign. Refreshment and a new focus is needed.
5. Become familiar with the many resource and game books useful in this work.
6. Be flexible. Alter your plans on a moment's notice.
7. While a team is performing, the teacher must observe audience reactions as well as the play work. The interaction of the audience is part of the creative dramatics experience.
8. Avoid giving examples. Too often the students become bound to that example and don't try new things.
9. If the environment in the workshop is joyous and free of authoritarianism, everyone will "play" and become as open as young children.

Cooperative Group Activities Using Creative Drama

1. Personification: A Prewriting Activity

Each student draws the name of an inanimate object (pencil sharpener, doorknob, waste basket, alarm clock, etc.). Students pick a partner and develop an improvisation.

2. Showing Emotions

Assign a "emotion" to each student (anger, jealousy, shyness, nervousness, nerdiness, arrogance, etc.). Students must act out the emotion without actually naming or referring to it. The class notes significant details and discusses which emotion was being portrayed.

3. Using Drama To Extend a Story

Creative drama can extend a story. Try "blocking" a play as you read it aloud in class. Giving a visual perspective increases concentration.

4. Increasing Research and Journalism Skills

Using techniques of role playing and creative drama, have student groups show *how* to interview (Give good and bad examples.) Short excerpts from TV news or radio information programs provide good models for discussion and creative drama activities.

6. Use Creative Drama to Increase Vocabulary

Assign five words to a group and let them use them in a skit.

7. "Extend a Story"

Let students speculate on "what's next" in the life of a character based upon what we know from the literature.
Ask: "What happens to _____ next?"
Ask: "What if _____ and _____ met a year later . . . ?"
Ask: "What advice would _____ give to someone in a similar situation?" Have students act out what they think should go in the blank—or come up with a new ending to a story they already know.

8. Character Transpositions

Students can imagine the story they have just read in a town or city that they have seen. Take a character from some historical period and present him or her with a dilemma of the 1980s. Design a skit around one of these situations.

The King Arthur Tales:
• Merlin working in a used car lot.
• Lancelot at a rock concert.
• Guenevere at a NOW meeting.
• Arthur interviewing for a job on Wall Street

9. Send students back through time . . .

The Crucible:
• What happens to an eighties' teenager (with Walkman & black T-shirt) who somehow lands in Salem at the height of the witch hysteria?

Within these activities students can be viewed as performers required to demonstrate their collective knowledge. The teacher's role is like that of a coach—helping students know and interpret the standards provoking thought.

The Language Arts and Creative Thinking Skills

Creative drama and writing are good ways for students to share imaginative ideas with their peers, creating an atmosphere where unconscious thought can flow freely. Exploring how community or historical figures developed their ability to think imaginatively can help. The following are elements to look for in creative thinking:

• *Fluency*	• Producing and considering many alternatives.
• *Originality*	• Producing ideas which go beyond the obvious and are unique and valued.
• *Highlighting the essence.*	• Finding and expressing the main idea.
• *Elaboration:*	• Filling out an idea or set of ideas by adding details.
• *Keeping Open:*	• Delaying closure, seeing many ideas, considering a range of information, making mental leaps.
• *Awareness of Emotions*	• Developing and expressing emotional awareness, perseverance, involvement, and commitment.

• *Combining and Synthesizing:*	• Seeing relationships and joining parts and elements to form a whole.
• *Visualizing— Richly and Colorfully:*	• Perceiving and creating images which are vivid, strong and alive.
• *Visualizing— The Inside:*	• Seeing and presenting ideas and objects from an internal vantage point.
• *Enjoying and Using Fantasy*	• Making use of imagination in a playful way.
• *Using Movement:*	• Learning, thinking, and communicating kinesthetically.
• *Using Sound*	• Interpreting and communicating ideas, concepts, and feelings through sound and music.
• *Breaking through and Extending Boundaries*	• Overcoming limitations and conventions and creating new solutions.
• *Using Humor*	• Combining incongruous situations with comical wit, surprise and amusement.
• *Imagining the Future*	• Envisioning alternatives, predicting consequences, and planning ahead.

Students learn elements of creative thinking from interpersonal group behaviors. Cooperative groups can help develop these and other language skills in a variety of ways: listening, speaking, arguing, problem solving and clarifying; so does having pairs of students argue an issue with other pairs, then switching sides. The chaos and dissonance of group work can actually foster critical thinking and imaginative language development. We must learn to work creatively with conflicts, viewing them as possibilities for the cooperative improvement of education.

> *Dust as we are, the immortal spirit grows,*
> *Like harmony in music;*
> *There is a dark inscrutable workmanship*
> *that reconciles discordant elements,*
> *Makes them cling together in one society.*
> —Wordsworth[31]

When teachers change both the nature of the materials used in the instruction and the way they organize the classroom, they need the

31. Wordsworth, W.: The Prelude: In *English Romantic Writers*. D. Perkins (Ed.). New York, Harcourt Brace Jovanovich, 1967.

"I Burned the Planet, Dear"

Figure 9. Contains a digitized element from a painting by Jody Mussoff.

cooperation of administrators, parents and teacher educators. In our view, language arts instruction must be a satisfying experience for all learners. Along with reading comprehension, writing and creative experience goes developing the capacity for aesthetic response. Collaborative language inquiry can provide a challenge and a sense of efficacy. Intrinsically engaging activities can help students develop the right habits of the mind. The process needs teachers who are adventurous leaders, capable of promoting high levels of engagement and cooperation.

REFERENCES

Adams, D., & Hamm, M. *Media and Literacy: Learning In an Electronic Age.* Springfield, IL: Charles C Thomas, 1989.

Adams, D. "Interactive Children's Literature." *Reading Horizons,* 1986.

Adams, D. "What Children Read Influences How They Write." *The Leaflet.* NCTE, 1984.

Ashton, P. T., & Rodman, B.W.: *Making a Difference: Teachers Sense of Efficacy and Student Achievement.* New York: Longman, 1986.

Bartel, R.: *Metaphors and Symbols.* Urbana, IL: National Council of Teachers of English, 1983.

Bruffee, K. A.: "Collaborative Learning and the Conversation of Mankind." *College English.* Vol. 46., 1984.

Bruner, J.: *Actual Minds, Possible Worlds.* Cambridge, MA: Harvard University Press, 1986.

Bruner, J. Goodnow, J., & Austin, G.: *A Study of Thinking.* New Brunswick, NJ, Transaction Books, 1986.

Burns, P., Roe, B., & Ross, E.: *Teaching Reading in Today's Elementary Schools.* Boston, Houghton Mifflin, 1988.

Cazden, C.: *Classroom Discourse: The Language of Teaching and Learning.* Portsmouth, NH: Heinemann, 1988.

Coles, R.: *The Moral Life of Children.* Boston, Atlantic Monthly Press, 1986.

Conley, M.: *Grouping Within Reach.* Newark, DE, International Reading Association, 1987.

Cooper, C. R. (Ed.): *Researching Response to Literature and the Teaching of Literature.* Norwood, NJ, Ablex, 1985.

Cushenbery, D.: *Comprehensive Reading Strategies for All Secondary Students.* Springfield, Charles C Thomas, 1988.

Davidson, J.L. (Ed.): *Counterpoint and Beyond.* Urbana, IL: National Council of Teachers of English, 1988.

Davidson, J., & Koppenhaver, D.: *Adolescent Literacy: What Works Best and Why.* New York, Garland Publishing, 1989.

Denman, G.: *When You've Made It Your Own...; Teaching Poetry to Young People.* Portsmouth, NH, Heinemann Educational Books, 1989.

Easthope, A.: *Poetry and Phantasy.* Cambridge, Cambridge University Press, 1988.

Ennis, R.: "A Taxonomy of Critical Thinking Dispositions and Abilities." In *Teaching Thinking Skills: Theory and Practice.* J. Boyokoff Baron & R. Sternberg (Eds.). New York, W.H. Freeman & Co., 1987.

Gardner, R.: *Metacognition and Reading Comprehension.* Norwood, NJ, Ablex, 1987.

Gere, A. R. (Ed.): *Roots in the Sawdust: Writing to Learn Across the Disciplines.* Urbana, IL, National Council of Teachers of English, 1985.

Graves, D.: *Writing, Teachers and Children at Work.* Exeter, NH, Heinemann, 1983.

Haley, B. (Ed.). *Ideas Plus: Books 2, 3, 4, & 5 — A Collection of Practical Teaching Ideas.* Urbana, IL: National Council of Teachers of English, 1986.

Hansen, J.: *When Writers Read.* Portsmouth, NH, Hinemann, 1987.

Heilbrun, C.: *Writing A Woman's Life.* New York, Norton, 1989.

Hirsch, E.D., Kett, J., & Trefil, J.: *The Dictionary of Cultural Literacy.* Houghton, Mifflin, 1988.

Hladczuck, J., & Elter, W.: *Comparative Reading: An International Bibliography.* Westport, CT, Greenwood Press, 1987.

Hollander, J.: *Melodious Guile: Fictive Pattern in Poetic Language.* New Haven, CT, Yale University Press, 1989.

Johnson, K.: *Doing Words: Using the Creative Power of Children's Personal Images to Teach Reading and Writing.* Boston, Houghton Mifflin, 1987.

Johnson, P.H.: "Teachers as Evaluation Experts: A Cognitive Basis" *The Reading Teacher.* April, 744–48.

Marcel, A., & Carpenter, P.: *The Psychology of Reading and Language Comprehension.* Newton, MA, Allen and Bacon, 1987.

Nagy, W. E.: *Teaching Vocabulary to Improve Reading Comprehension.* Urbana, IL: National Council of Teachers of English, 1988.

Nell, V.: *Lost in a Book.* New Haven, CT, Yale University Press, 1989.

Newman, S.: *Television and Reading: A Research Synthesis.* ERIC ED 267 389.

Oakes, J.: *Keeping Track: How Schools Structure Inequity.* New Haven, Yale University Press, 1985.

Perfetti, C.: *Reading Ability.* New York, Oxford University Press, 1985. *Puppet tools.* Box 3200 Richmond, VA: Prescott/Durrell Program, 1988.

Reinking, D. (Ed.): *Reading and Computers: Issues for Theory and Practice.* New York, Teachers College Press, 1987.

Resnick, L.: Education and Learning To Think. Report. Washington, D.C., National Academy Press, 1987.

Smith, F.: *Reading Without Nonsense.* New York, Teachers College Press, 1985.

Solomon, P., & Claire, H.: *Classroom Collaboration.* London, Routledge & Kagan, 1984.

Sternberg, R. J.: Teaching critical thinking: Are we making critical mistakes? *Phi Delta Kappan,* 67, 1985.

Stotsky, S.: *Holistic Scoring of School-based Writing.* ERIC #196011.

Timar, T., and Kirp, D.: *Managing Educational Excellence.* New York, Falmer Press, 1988.

Tsujimoto, J. I.: *Teaching Poetry Writing to Adolescents.* Urbana, IL, National Council of Teachers of English, 1988.

Vygotsky, L. *Thought and Language.* Cambridge, MA, MIT Press, 1986.

Weintraub, S. (Ed.): *Summary of Investigations Relating To Reading.* Newark, Delaware, International Reading Association, 1988.

Wordsworth, W.: The Prelude: In *English Romantic Writers.* D. Perkins, (Ed.). New York, Harcourt Brace Jovanovich, 1967.

5

COOPERATIVE LEARNING:
SCIENCE AND MATHEMATICS

There are all kinds of theories about why mathematics and science are so remarkably effective. My own view is that we're in the grip of an enormous teaching machine — the universe — which operates in essentially random ways. Random processes over billions of years, operating through natural selection, have produced birds and flowers and people. In the same way, there is a natural selection of ideas — which ideas work, which don't, what kind of thing is an appropriate description of nature. This process leads us to work together to develop mathematical and scientific ideas.

—Steven Weinberg

Mathematics and science have always revealed hidden patterns that help them understand the world. They are no longer just the building blocks of arcane academic domains. Now, they comprise an important part of a much larger framework of a technologically intensive society. More than ever, we must understand the basic outlines of math and science to solve unique problems, grasp patterns, and deal with the ambiguity of a constantly changing world. Citizens are increasingly called upon to participate in decisions ranging from nuclear power plants to genetically engineered life forms. Today's fast-paced technological and communications culture also requires workers who can go beyond machine calculations to think and solve and problems related to real-world situations.

Science and technology are having an increasing effect on education, the civic process, and American culture in general. In the next ten years, an estimated 70 percent of American jobs will be related somehow to the technology of computers and electronics. At the very time the importance of science and mathematics education is growing, most American students are pushed further and further from intelligent participation. Recent international comparisons rank American 5th graders 8th out of 17 countries in science achievement. By 9th grade we are in 15th place (out of 17) and sliding. Even advanced placement high school physics students scored 9th and advanced chemistry students 11th on a 13-country comparison. Results on mathematics tests are similar. American 8th grade students scored well below other countries in solving problems that require analysis and higher levels of thinking.[1]

Adding to the problem of declining test scores is demographic change. Minority students and women simply aren't studying much math and science. Research recently gathered by the U.S. Education Department found a majority of girls, disadvantaged students and minorities are lost to these subjects by the time they leave elementary school. Lack of effective instruction and loss of student interest are major factors in this loss of talent.

To improve science and mathematics education for *all* students requires new approaches. There is also a mismatch today between the science and mathematics curriculum found in schools and that which most students want and need for "real-world" activities. Current curricula largely consist of textbooks, teacher talk and testing in spite of general agreement that math and science curriculum for the 1990s should emphasize thinking skills and model methods of cooperative inquiry.[2] New programs should not be just reading the textbook but an active group examination of the nature of science, the influence of technology, and the needs of the students' community.

Understanding How Children Learn

Problems in learning mathematics and science are the major factors that push students to fail in school. Much of the failure is due to a tradition of teaching that is inappropriate with the way students learn. Cognitive psychologists, such as Piaget and Bruner, explain that students construct understandings based on their own experiences and that each individual's knowledge of math and science is personal.[3] Yet, the least effective mode for math and science teaching still prevails in many classrooms. Science and mathematics lessons where students are expected to read, listen and memorize abstract concepts or symbolic procedures are common. Besides leaving a bad taste for the subject, students simply

---

1. National Assessment of Educational Progress, Washington, D.C., 1989.

2. Aronowitz, S.: *Science As Power: Discourse and Ideology in Modern Society.* Minneapolis, University of Minnesota Press.

3. Bruner, J., & Haste, H.: *Making Sense.* New York, Routledge, 1987.

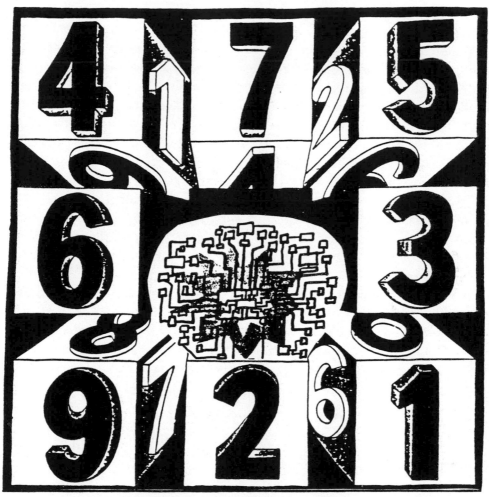

**Florida Commissioner of Education's 12-Point Plan
to Improve Math, Science and Computer Education**

1. Develop a corps of year-round math, science and computer-education teachers.
2. Develop extensive summer-school enhancement courses in math, science and computer education.
3. Require additional preservice education specifically designed for elementary math science teachers.
4. Require better textbooks and curriculum.
5. Develop regional magnet programs of excellence.
6. Focus teacher education on problem-centered, hands-on instruction.
7. Require that students be able to use calculators and computers to solve appropriate problems.
8. Begin a public awareness campaign, involving parents, business and educators, to encourage students to reduce time spent watching TV and spend more time on homework.
9. Develop special programs in math and science for girls and minorities.
10. Lengthen the elementary-school day to strengthen science education.
11. Determine appropriate math and science content of statewide testing programs.
12. Provide incentives for school districts to implement the comprehensive plan and encourage partnerships with business and parents.

Figure 10.

do not retain much of what they learn from lectures, worksheets, or doing more of the same as homework.

Teacher demonstrations, textbook pages, and repetition may help students do well on standardized tests. But these lower order skills are generally ineffective for long-term higher order thinking and problem solving. The results are abysmal when students are trained to search for right answers or hints of "how to do the page," rather than clear thinking, conceptual understanding or logical reasoning. The true goals of mathematics and science education are to help students learn how to apply knowledge, solve problems and promote understanding.

To really learn science and math, students must construct their own understandings, examine, represent, solve, transform, apply, prove, and communicate. This happens most effectively when students work in groups to discuss, make presentations, invent or create their own theories. Such an environment encourages students to engage in a great deal of invention as they impose their interpretation on what is presented and create theories that makes sense to them. Learning about science and mathematics also involves learning to think critically and create relationships. How these relationships are structured in a student's mind depends on such factors as maturity, physical experience, and social interactions.

Cooperative Learning Experiences

Learning about math and science is enhanced when students are given opportunities to explain their own ideas, interact with others, explore, question, and try out new approaches. There is substantial evidence that students working in groups can master science and mathematics material better than students working alone.[4] The more opportunities students have for social interaction, the more divergent viewpoints and perspectives can season their thinking. Through collaborative group explorations students can be pushed to analyze what they think, discuss it, and clarify their own reasoning. Working in small groups also gives students a chance to interact with concepts and verbalize their conceptions within a relatively safe situation. And learning environments where working together is part of the classroom "culture" encourage more participation with less worry about being wrong.

As most teachers know from experience, cooperative group work is

4. Slavin, R.: *School and Classroom Organization.* Hillsdale, NJ, Erlbaum 1989.

more than pushing some desks together. Students must have a reason to take one another's progress seriously and care about the team's success. This develops most fully when students are engaged in active group learning where they stand or fall together. If the group task is simply to complete a worksheet, the easiest approach may be to let the highest-achieving students do most of the work. Suggestions or questions from low achieving students may be pushed aside as interfering with efficiency. Active cooperation is different. Rather than having group success based on a single product, it is the sum of individual learning performances of all members. Collaborative goals are based on *all* group members learning and *doing.*

A Cooperative Learning Model for Teaching Science and Mathematics

Cognitive views of learning that emphasize prior knowledge and thinking processes within the learner suggest that changes need to be made in the ways that educators think about learners, teaching, and organizing the school classroom.[5] Central to creating such an learning environment is the desire to help individuals acquire or construct knowledge. The underlying concept is that knowledge is to be shared or developed— rather than held by the authority. This holds teachers to a high standard, for they must have both subject matter knowledge and pedagogical knowledge based on an understanding of cognitive and developmental processes.

The cooperative learning model for science and math that we suggest here emphasizes the benefits of learning rather than external rewards for academic performance. Lessons are introduced with statements concerning reasons for engaging in the learning task—reasons like learning to think critically or exploring the nature of an interesting topic. Students are encouraged to assume responsibility for learning and evaluating their own work and the work of others. Interaction may include a discussion of the validity of explanations, the search for more information, the testing of various explanations or consideration of the pros and cons of specific decisions.

The characteristics that distinguish new collaborative math and science learning settings from old textbook and lecture models revolve

---

5. Paul, R., Binker, K. Jensen, K., & Kreklau, H.: *Critical Thinking Handbook.* Rohnert Park, CA, Sonoma State University, 1989.

around group goals and the accompanying benefits of active group work. Instead of being told they need information, students learn to recognize when additional data is needed. They jointly seek it out, apply it, they see its power and value. In this way the actual *use* of science and mathematics information becomes the starting point rather than an add on. The teacher facilitates the process, instead of acting as a knowledge dispenser. Student success is measured on performance, work samples, application or synthesis. Simple recall is not as important.

A Model of Mathematics and Science Instruction:
Characteristics of Textbook and Cooperative Learning Settings

Model Characteristic	Traditional Textbook Model	Mathematics and Science Active Learning Model
Theory	Behavioristic rewards/grades	Cognitive internal/self enhancement
Goals	product	process, learning, knowledge
Method	textbook, lecture memorization	joint group project inquiry, research skills
Skills	memorization presenting a problem, reporting	communication, negotiation resolving, presenting alternative solutions
Student's role	knowledge recipient	student as researcher reporting, synthesizing
Teacher's role	teacher as expert	teacher as learner
Authority	teacher	individual/shared
Evaluation	external	joint
Learning Setting	competition teacher validates thinking, recitation	collaboration self-reliance group reliance higher level thinking

Common themes of a cooperative science and mathematics learning model include an emphasis on exploring a problem, thinking, and the collaborative challenge of posing a solution. Cooperative learning is central to the process. This involves peer helping, self-evaluation, and group support for risk-taking. This also means accepting individual differences and having positive expectations for everyone in the group. Students understand the purpose of their tasks as contributing to their own learning and self-development. If the teacher can help children push these elements together, the result will be greater persistence and more self-directed learning. To reach these goals also requires viewing classrooms as learning places where teaching methods build on cognitive perspectives rather than coercion.

ORGANIZING THE COOPERATIVE LEARNING SCIENCE AND MATHEMATICS CLASSROOM

Getting started with cooperative learning in math and science means defining student and teacher responsibilities. Changing the classroom organization frequently requires change in the physical structure. Mixed-ability learning groups of four students have proven effective in mathematics and science classes.[6] This may mean adding work tables or pushing chairs together to form comfortable work spaces that are conducive to open communication. It is important to involve students in establishing rules for active group work. Rules should be kept simple and might include the following:

- Everyone is responsible for his or her own work.
- Each person is responsible for his or her own behavior.
- Everyone must be willing to help anyone who asks.
- Ask the teacher for help when no one in the group can answer the question.

Group roles and individual responsibilities also need to be clearly defined. And if the learning activities require materials, students may be required to take responsibility for assembling and storing them.

The Role of the Teacher

In a cooperative learning classroom teachers need to provide time for students to grapple with problems, try out strategies, discuss, experiment, explore and evaluate. Because the primary focus is on the students' own investigations, discussions, and group projects, the teacher's role shifts to one analogous to that of a team coach or expert manager.

---

6. Burns, M.: *The Good Times Math Event Book.* Oak Lawn, IL, Creative Publications, 1977.

Teachers need to model attitudes and present themselves as problem solvers and models of inquiry. They do this by letting students know that everyone is an active learner and no one knows all the answers. Teachers also need to exhibit an interest in finding solutions to problems, show confidence in trying various strategies, and risk being wrong. It is more important to emphasize the aspect of *working on the problem* than getting "the answer." By creating a safe environment, where students are encouraged and affirmed teachers can push the boundaries of the curriculum into new spaces.

Teaching the Cooperative Group Lesson

When teaching a lesson, it is important that students understand the problem situation and work together to find and evaluate the solution. Specific strategies are helpful in each of these steps.

Introducing the Lesson

During the initial introduction the teacher's objective is for the students to understand the problem or skill and establish guidelines for the group's work. The teacher presents or reviews the necessary concepts or skills with the whole class and poses a part of the problem or an example of a problem for the class to try. Opportunities for discussion are provided. The actual group problem is then presented after the conceptual overview. The class is encouraged to discuss and clarify the problem task. Before breaking the class into groups it is helpful to have a student or two explain the problem back to the class in their own words. This summary of the teacher's directions can help clarify, define and set up the group task. This also helps the teacher promote thinking skills and ensure an understanding of the problem task. Students then break into small learning groups as assigned.

Group Exploration

Students work cooperatively to solve the problem. The teacher observes, listens to the groups' ideas, and offers assistance as needed. The teacher is also responsible for providing extension activities when a group is done early. If a group is having difficulties, the teacher helps them discover what they know so far, poses a simple example or perhaps points out a misconception or erroneous idea of the group. Sometimes a group has trouble getting along or focusing on what they are supposed to be doing. At this time it may be necessary to refocus the group's attention by asking questions such as: What are you supposed to be doing? What is the task? How will you get organized? What materials do you need? Who will do what?

Summarizing

After the problem task and group exploration are completed students again meet as a whole class to summarize and present their findings. Groups present their solutions and share their processes. When the processes are shared, both group procedures and problem-solving strategies are summarized.

Questions might include: How did you organize the task? What problems did you have? What method did you use? Was your group method effective? Did anyone have a different method or strategy for solving the problem? Do you think your solution makes sense? Encourage students to generalize from their results. What other problem does this remind you of? What other follow-up experiment could you try based on your findings? Students are encouraged to listen to and respond to other students' comments. It may also be helpful to make notes of the responses on the chalkboard to help summarize the class data at the close of the lesson.

A Beginning Cooperative Activity

Cooperative group learning in math and science allows students to participate in activities that serve as a basis for observation as well as reflection. Math and science activities frequently center around general principles relating to the topic being studied. Students are asked to explore problems and form generalizations that direct their applications in new situations.[7] The pooling of tasks, exercises, and games involves students directly in cooperative interactions with their peers. Cooperative experiential learning activities involve concrete experiences, observation, making generalizations, reflection, the forming of concepts, and testing or applying concepts to new situations.

---

7. Chickering, A. *Experience and Learning.* Rochelle, NY, Change Magazine Press, 1977.

Concrete Experience

In this beginning group activity students are asked to survey the group and prepare a group poster or graph which reflects the ideas of every member of the class. This exposes the group to a range of cooperative procedures. The group must exchange ideas (What do we want to find out? What will it look like? What topic should we choose?) and share feelings (What are we going to do? How do we organize it?). Lack of specific instructions can lead to frustration in some individuals. Members must help each other organize, plan, and produce a product. Each group presents their work to the class and reports on how their group arrived at the finished product. Hanging the graphs and posters creates a sense of belonging as a group.

Observation and Reflection

Learners reflect on the experience's significance for them. This is a bridge between the experience and formal learning role as observers. Students are asked to examine these questions:

- *What happened in your group?* Students share perceptions with each other. This allows them to recognize that not all members perceive the event the same.
- *How did the group participants feel?* (Positive, negative, trust and acceptance factors are revealed as well as elements of "risk" and exposure.)
- *What does it mean?* Students explore meaning, generalize, and examine group roles.

Formalization of abstract concepts and generalizations

To help students interpret the knowledge gained through the experience and as a guide to application, teachers may wish to assign follow-up readings, activities, or assignments which involve the use of surveys, graphing, or data presentation.

Testing Applications in new situations

Based on what they found out students may wish to choose a new topic to study or create new group tasks with a real-world emphasis. The more complex the thinking and the higher order processing of information, the greater the effect on problem-solving social skills and attitudes.

HOW EXEMPLARY TEACHERS
MANAGE THE COOPERATIVE CLASSROOM

To be most effective, teaching must respond to students' prior knowledge and ideas. This means that teachers need to *listen* as much as they speak—resisting the temptation to control classroom ideas so that students can get some sense of ownership over their own learning. In a cooperative classroom a give and take exists between students and teachers and students and students. This involves open discussion and honest criticism of ideas.

Studies of exemplary teachers reveal strategies which facilitated sustained student engagement. These teachers were very successful at *controlling at a distance.* Moving around the room and speaking with individuals and groups from time to time was also part of the repertoire of teachers who were identified as good role models.[8] Students were able to work independently and cooperatively in groups as they developed a surprising degree of autonomy and independence. In classrooms identified as exemplary, students demonstrated the capacity to work together when problems arose, and they knew when to seek help from a peer or the teacher. Teachers were not always worried about maintaining order, nor were they rushing from one student to another (on demand) as hands went up. These teachers had considered all the possibilities and even had time to reflect on the lesson as it progressed. The key to successful monitoring was establishing routines that enabled the teachers to cope with a number of diverse learning needs. In all cases an active student role was emphasized and activities were prescribed to ensure that students were active mentally. And when difficulties were encountered students were encouraged to try to work them out for themselves, consult resources and peers.[9]

Many exemplary teachers also tended to explain task requirements. When off-task behavior occurred, the teacher quickly and quietly spoke to the individual, pairs or small groups concerned. They did so in a manner that did not disrupt the work of students who were on task. Model teachers also used strategies which encouraged students to actively participate in learning activities. Their safety nets, allowing students to

8. Tobin, K., & Fraser, B.: Case studies of exemplary science and mathematics teaching. *School Science and Mathematics*, 89(4), 1989.

9. Shulman, J., & Colbert, J.: *The Mentor Teacher Casebook*. ERIC Clearinghouse on Educational Management, 1987.

participate without embarrassment, were found to be especially beneficial among students who were relatively quiet. Although their classroom
atmosphere was often different, connecting learning with thinking and
understanding through the use of concrete materials was yet another
element that the most successful teachers had in common.

By encouraging verbal interactions among groups the teacher can
learn to monitor students' understanding of the content and occasionally
ask questions to stimulate thinking. By probing students' responses,
teachers in a cooperative learning environment can get students to
elaborate and clarify their thinking and speculations. Teachers can provide examples and additional information to groups when they are
stuck.[10] The most successful problem-solving approaches to learning
involved direct materials-centered experiences and assisted students in
developing critical thinking and interpersonal skills. Good teachers
used the features of a quality math and science program to maintain an
environment where students view these subjects in a favorable light.[11]

Combining Subject Matter and
Effective Instruction In a Technological Age

In math/science teaching both pedagogical and content area knowledge
are important. Without the essential content base teachers are unable to
focus students' thinking and unable to provide appropriate feedback or
effectively discuss the content. And without some knowledge of peda-
gogy it is difficult to make mathematics and science more personally
relevant and interesting for students.

Traditionally, there has been a gap between what was taught in science
and mathematics and what was really learned. Interpreting and understanding the real world—and how it relates to personal experience—is
different than the interpretations and understandings advanced in school
science and math courses. Typical school programs have produced students with increasingly negative attitudes about science and mathematics as they progress through the grades. This is especially true when
math and science courses do not consider needs, interests, motivations or

---

10. Meyer, C., & Sallee, T.: *Make It Simpler: A Practical Guide to Problem Solving in Mathematics.* Menlo Park, CA, Addison-Wesley, 1983.

11. Clark, C., Carter, B., & Sternberg, B.: *Math In Stride.* Menlo Park, CA, Addison-Wesley, 1988.

experiences of the learners, or when the material being covered is not viewed as useful or valuable.

The teaching of science and mathematics today requires a shifting of gears from a cognitive to a metacognitive stance. Students need to think skillfully and they need to be able to monitor their thinking processes as they work. Constructing a hypothesis, problem solving and cooperative group work can replace traditional chalk, talk and textbook methodology. It also helps to derive mathematics from each learner's reality and to pay attention to individual and group understanding. When these elements are in place, science and mathematics *can* be used to solve interesting problems in unique ways.

In teaching children to think scientifically and mathematically it is important to help them to apply their understanding and skills in solving problems, discovering relationships, analyzing patterns, generalizing relationships, and using numbers with confidence. Adding cooperative strategies can assist them in taking responsibility for their thoughts as they use higher level thinking skills and an inner confidence.

HOW SCIENCE AND MATH CAN
SHAPE THINKING AND VICE VERSA

Until this century, religion and philosophy were set in the past or in heaven. But progress in science and technology have (correctly or incorrectly) moved them to the near future on earth. Beginning early in this century, progress in science and its technological associates was viewed as capable of preventing hunger, disease, poverty, war, and even evil itself. Unfortunately, it didn't quite work out that way.

In spite of the limitations, technology has freed humanity from some of its more mundane tasks and changed in the process our relationship to physical and social reality. Recently, technological innovations, like calculators and computers, have changed the way science and mathematics are taught and learned. New models of instruction that encourage using technology and collaboration have sprung up to deal with this new aesthetic. We are now at a stage where teachers and students must move from seeing technology as a source of knowledge (coach, drill) to viewing it as a medium or forum for communication and intelligent adventure. Using technological innovations intelligently requires more thinking, problem formulating, and interpersonal communication skills.[12]

---

12. Forman, G., & Pufall, P. (Eds.): *Constructivism in the Computer Age.* Hillsdale, NJ, Lawrence Erlbaum, 1988.

Weird Science

Until the last few decades the best known scientists made use of every media forum to reach a mass audience. When Bertrand Russell was giving a public lecture on astronomy in 1920, he described how the earth orbits around the sun and how the sun, in turn, orbits around the center of a vast collection of stars called our galaxy. At the end of the lecture, a little old lady at the back of the room got up and said: "What you have told us is rubbish. The world is really a flat plate supported on the back of a giant tortoise." The scientist gave her a superior smile before replying, "What is the tortoise standing on?" "You're very clever, young man, very clever," said the old lady. "But it's turtles all the way down."

—Russell-Hawkins

Figure 11.

A substantive knowledge base now exists regarding the social and psychological characteristics of how children learn about mathematics, science and technology. Yet, studies indicate that even experienced teachers are not familiar with this knowledge.[13] The challenge is to make research-based knowledge accessible to both practicing teachers and students in teacher education programs.

We are just beginning to examine some of the factors that shape mathematical behavior. It's becoming increasingly clear that being able to think scientifically and mathematically requires more than large amounts of exposure to content. Students need direct decision-making experiences so that their minds can be broadened by applying science and mathematics. By actively examining and solving problems, students can become flexible and resourceful as they use their knowledge efficiently and come to understand the rules which underlie these domains of knowledge.

Shoenfeld (1985) examined traditional programs and found that students' foundations (cognitive resources) for problem solving far weaker than their performance on tests would indicate. His studies suggested that even mathematically talented high school and college students (who experienced success in upper division math courses) had little or no awareness of how to use math heuristics (rules of thumb). When faced with nonstandard problems which were not put in a textbook context (oriented toward solutions), students experienced failures and ended up doing distracting calculations and trivia instead of applying the basic concepts at their disposal.[14] Even students who received good grades in memory-based programs frequently had serious misconceptions about mathematics and science. Implementing well-learned mechanical procedures in domains where little is understood is one thing—deep learning of a subject is quite another. The best science and mathematics instruction also leaves space for a child's mind to play.

Social and Environmental Factors
That Influence How Math and Science Are Learned

The difficulties the American educational system is having in teaching science and mathematics points to yet another problem. The substance of the subject matter we teach, which is the focus of nearly all of our attention in the classroom, determines only part of what our stu-

---

13. Carey, N., Mittman, B. & Darling-Hammand, L.: *Recruiting Mathematics and Science Teachers Through Nontraditional Programs: A Survey.* Santa Monica, CA, Rand Corporation, 1989.

14. Shoenfeld, A.: *Mathematical Problem Solving.* Orlando, FL, Academic Press, 1985.

dents learn. The home and social environment plays a central role in determining what students extract from their math and science lessons.[15]

When some groups are put off the subject and when instruction focuses almost entirely on the mastery of facts, many students are not likely to develop some of the higher order thinking skills necessary for using math and science. If we want students to learn critical thinking and problem-solving skills, then we must focus on the development of these skills. An effective problem solver brings her own substantive knowledge and experience to a problem and then applies features of this knowledge to the situations under study.

We need to change our thinking about how to teach science and mathematics. Education is one issue. Another is that skills taught in isolation lead to isolated thinking and infrequent use in real-world situations. There is a need for science and mathematics to be integrated with language arts, visual and performing arts, social studies, movement, and technology. Understanding the need for all children to talk and think scientifically and mathematically is equally important if we are to enter a more mature period in human history.

One of the most important conclusions of the current research on higher order thinking skills is that transfer of skills from one area to another does not occur automatically. Some students intuitively see connections between mathematics, science, and critical thinking, others do not. For many, generalizations must be planned or may not occur. The research suggests that if teachers are aware of and actively promote generalizations, transfer to real-world situations will be more likely. Learning moves along a path from concrete experiences to abstract manipulations. An important instructional principal, strongly validated by recent educational research, is children learn science and mathematics more effectively when they can concretely experience the principles they are studying.[16]

The success factor is strongly related to the amount of learning that takes place in studying math and science. Even if students are actively engaged, they learn most effectively only when they are performing mental activities with reasonable rates of success. In the math classroom students' efficiency of learning is also related to the extent

15. Kaseverg, A., Kreinberg, N., & Downie, D.: *Use EQUALS to Promote the Participation of Women In Mathematics.* Berkeley, CA, Lawrence Hall of Science, 1980.

16. Langbort, C., & Thompson, V.: *Building Success in Math.* Belmont, CA, Wadsworth, Publishing, 1985.

that their class and study time is turned into academic learning time. This means the longer students actively attend to a task, the higher the rate of success.[17]

PROBLEM SOLVING IN THE MATH/SCIENCE CLASSROOM AND IN THE WORLD

We live in a complex time where personal and global problems confront us daily. Preventing a nuclear war, preserving our national resources, population control, terrorism, and drug use are only a handful of the major difficulties confronting our society on a regular basis. Problem solutions are elusive.

Skill in cooperatively solving problems is one of the most essential and valuable tools that we can teach. No topic presented in schools can be more vital or pertinent than problem solving. Yet, acquisition of this skill, despite good intentions of school personnel, remains tentative at best. Problem solving goes beyond a subject or discipline by requiring a facility with language, thinking, and a general understanding of the world.

In the process of solving a problem, memory, collaboration, critical and creative thinking merge in order to identify, analyze and evaluate responses and products. Thinking scientifically and mathematically involves representing world phenomena by mental constructs, searching for the optimal solution, asking the "what if" questions, and extending natural language to symbolic representation. In these decision-making situations alternatives must be weighed and the consequences of various solutions examined. Communicating with computations means maximizing efficiency, inferring, reasoning from data, finding connections, analyzing and searching for explanations. These functions of science and mathematics cannot be taken for granted.

Actual problems, found outside of school, have little to do with the information found in many textbooks or in most school lesson plans. Yet, such problem solving is a part of everyday experience; it usually starts with problem identification, proceeds to problem resolution and involves decision making. Schools can help. Whether it's with concrete materials or visually intensive electronic tools, well-prepared teachers can involve students in experiences which transcend the classroom and the school.

---

17. Stenmark, J., Thompson, V., & Cossey, R.: *Family Math.* Palo Alto, CA, Dale Seymour Press, 1986.

Since much on-the-job application requires a response to rapidly changing problems, specific skill training can be very limiting. Forging ahead with curriculum models without examining the future needs of students in the workplace can be shortsighted and self-defeating. There is a natural human tendency to do things that are viewed as having some general utility. Many students don't see the point in mastering material that is detached from the world outside of school.

In school, students usually do math alone—without tools (like calculators). In the world of work they usually work together in agenda-setting groups using any tools they can get their hands on. (In school that's often called cheating.)

Classrooms can be organized so that small mixed-ability groups are a forum for math/science discussions, discovery and creativity. When students resourcefully collaborate, ask questions and explore possible answers, they can develop an energetic enthusiasm about these subjects. As mathematics and science move from their computational and factual base to a problem-solving emphasis, these subjects can come alive and stimulate students because of their immediacy.

COLLABORATION ACTIVITIES FOR MATH AND SCIENCE

Learning is enhanced by presenting information in multiple formats, including multisensory activities and experimental opportunities. Some of these include concrete manipulatives like geopieces, cuisinaire rods, blocks, fraction pieces, base ten blocks, popsicle sticks, chips, etc. Other activities include TV programs, computer simulations, role-playing problems and instructional courseware. These cooperative group activities have proved highly motivational and effective at reaching multiple learning styles.

1. Math/Science Scavenger Hunt (elementary)

Mathematics and science applications are all around us. Mathematical patterns in nature abound. Architecture, art and everyday objects rely heavily on mathematical principles, patterns, and symmetrical geometric form. Students need to see and apply real-world connections to concepts in science and mathematics. This activity is designed to get students involved and more aware of the mathematical/scientific relationships all around them and to use technology to help report their findings.

Divide the class into four groups. Each group is directed to find and bring back as many objects as they can that meet the requirements on their list. Some objects may need to be sketched out on paper if they are too difficult to bring back to the classroom, but encourage them to try to bring back as many as possible

Group One: Measurement Hunt

Find and bring back objects that are:

- as wide as your hand
- further away than you can throw
- half the size of a baseball
- smaller than your little finger
- thinner than a shoelace
- a foot long
- waist high
- as long as your arm
- wider than four people
- as wide as your nose

Group Two: Shape Hunt

Find and bring back as many objects as you can that have these shapes:

- triangle • circle • square • diamond • oval
- rectangle • hexagon • other geometric shapes

Group Three: Number Pattern Hunt

Find objects that show number patterns. For example, a three-leaf clover matches the number pattern three.

Group Four: Textures

Find as many objects as you can that have the following characteristics:

- smooth • rough • soft • grooved/ridges
- hard • bumpy • furry • sharp • wet • grainy

When students return, have them arrange their objects in some type of order or classification. Using a graphing program on the computer or colored paper, scissors and markers, have them visually represent their results in some way (bar graph, for example).

2. Student-Generated Problems

Have student groups construct their own problems on a topic of their choice. Encourage them to use survey data, newspaper stories, or current information (TV guide is one source). Encourage calculator use.

3. Surveys and Graphing

Divide the class into small groups of four or five. Have them brainstorm about what they would like to find out from the other class members (favorite hobbies, TV shows, kinds of pets, etc.). Once a topic is agreed upon and OK'd by the teacher, have them organize and take a survey of all of the class members. Remember, several groups will be doing this at once, so allow for some noise and movement. When the statistics are gathered and compiled, each group must make a clear descriptive graph which can be posted in the classroom. Encourage originality and creativity.

4. Global Problem Statistics (middle school)

Charts and graphs are visual communication forms that reveal statistical data at a glance. These visual models can help lead to a better understanding of global problems and real-world situations. Using world population statistics and calculators have student groups made comparisons between land size and population. Some sample activities:

1. Graph the regions by size according to population and land size.
2. Calculate how many people per square kilometer in each continent. Chart your answer.
3. Describe what you can infer about each continent by looking at these statistics.
4. Look up annual food production for a region of your choice. Write a description of how this compares to its land size and population.

World Population by Region

region	population	area (sq km)
Africa	412,000,000	30,319,000
North America	239,000,000	21,515,000
South America	333,000,000	20,566,000
Asia	2,304,000,000	27,580,000
Europe	476,000,000	4,937,000
Oceania	21,700,000	8,510,000
U.S.S.R.	258,000,000	22,402,000

5. Collecting TV Data

Have students survey their families' viewing habits. The survey questions could follow the same format as the Nielson survey data. This kind of survey includes what programs are watched, what time the TV is on, how many people are watching at a time, etc. Compose the survey instrument with the class based on information they would like to find out. (A note to parents outlining the intent of the activity and the assignment is helpful.) After the students have gathered the data for a week's time, have them summarize the information in their group. Compare such items as the average time spent watching TV for the group, most popular times for watching, most popular shows, etc. These are excellent ways to integrate charts and graphs into the technology curriculum. This kind of activity can also lead into social education and values clarification activities. Questions can be explored such as: How much TV viewing is good? What other things do you give up when you spend time watching television? How much talking goes on while the TV set is on? Ask for volunteers to spend one week not watching television. This group should keep a record of what they did instead of watch television. Encourage volunteers to share their reactions to the experiment with the class.

6. Mathematics and Science In the World of Work

Have students gather information about mathematics and science in the workplace and careers that spark their interest. Draw up a simple survey form listing occupations that students are interested in, and spaces to gather data about ways mathematics and science is used on the job. Have student groups interview workers, parents, community professionals, and friends to find out how they use science and mathematics tools in their work. Have groups assemble and display the data in visual form (charts, graphs, etc.). Look for patterns and comparisons. Are there generalizations that can be made? Conclusions that can be drawn?

7. Using Community Resources

Museums are one way to link science and community resources. Students can play the role of curators. Working in pairs have students investigate objects such as bones, fossils, shells, etc. Have students find out all they can about the object using the full range of resources available at the museum or naturalist center.

To add an element of interest and adventure, have students in groups of four create a fictitious but plausible scenario to accompany an object of their choice. In one story students were told the bone was brought to them by the FBI who expressed concern that it might be human. (The Smithsonian actually gets many such cases each year.) Student groups must try to determine the origin, if not a human bone, then they are to find what animal the bone belonged to, what part of the skeleton, etc. At the end of the activity, student groups return to the class and present their problem and the findings.

8. Bridge Building

This is an interdisciplinary activity which reinforces skills of communication, group process, social studies, language arts, mathematics, science and technology.

Materials:

Lots of newspaper and masking tape, one large, heavy rock, and one cardboard box. Have students bring in stacks of newspapers. You need approximately one foot of newspaper per person. Bridges are a tribute to technological efforts which employ community planning, engineering efficiency, mathematical precision, aesthetics, group effort, and construction expertise.

Procedures:

1. For the first part of this activity, divide students into three groups. Each group will be responsible for investigating one aspect of bridge building.

Group One: Research

This group is responsible for going to the library and looking up facts about bridges, collecting pictures of kinds of bridges, and bringing back information to be shared with the class.

Group Two: Aesthetics, Art, Literature

This group must discover songs, books about bridges, paintings, artwork, etc. which deals with bridges.

Group Three: Measurement, Engineering

This group must discover design techniques, blueprints, angles, and measurements, of actual bridge designs. If possible, visit a local bridge to look at the structural design, etc. Each group presents their findings to the class. The second part of this activity involves actual bridge construction by the students.

2. Assemble the collected stacks of newspaper, tape, the rock and the box at the front of the room. Divide the class into groups of four or five students. Each group is instructed to take an even portion of newspaper to their group and one or two rolls of masking tape. Explain that the group will be responsible for building a stand-alone bridge using only the newspapers and tape. The bridge is to be constructed so that it will support the large rock and so that the box can pass underneath.

3. Each group is given three to five minutes of planning time in which they are allowed to talk and plan together. During the planning time they are not allowed to touch the newspapers and tape, but they are encouraged to pick up the rock and make estimates of how high the box is.

4. At the end of the planning time students are given 10 to 12 minutes to build their bridge. During this time there is no talking among the group members. They may not handle the rock or the box, only the newspapers and tape. (A few more minutes may be necessary to ensure that all groups have a chance of finishing their constructions.)

Evaluation:

Stop all groups after the allotted time. Survey the bridges with the class and allow each group to try to pass the two tests for their bridge. (Does the bridge support the rock and does the box fit underneath?) Discuss the design of each bridge and how they compare to the bridges researched earlier.

Follow up/Enrichment

As a follow-up activity, have each group measure their bridge and design a blueprint, (include angles, length and width of the bridge) so that another group could build the bridge by following this model.

9. Building Visual Models: Concept Circles and Venn Diagrams

Science teachers can make use of a variety of diagrams to help students grasp important concepts. Like mapping, concept circles demonstrate meaning and develop visual thinking. Have student groups represent their understanding of science concepts by constructing concept circles following these rules:

1. Let a circle represent any concept (plant, weather, bird . . .)
2. Print the name of that concept inside the circle.
3. When you want to show that one concept is included within another concept, draw a smaller circle within a larger circle. For example, large circle planets, smaller circle earth.
4. To demonstrate that some elements of one concept are part of another concept, draw partially overlapping circles. Label each. (Water contains some minerals.) The relative size of the circles can show the level of specificity for each concept. Bigger circles can be used for more general concepts or used to represent relative amounts.
5. To show two concepts are not related, draw two separate non-connected circles and label each one. (bryophytes—mosses, without true leaves, tracheophytes—vascular plants with leaves, stems, and roots)

10. Playing With Sound

Play is important not only in the development of intelligence of children but emerges over and over as an important step in invention and discovery. Curiosity, play, following hunches is particularly important in developing one of the most valuable scientific tools: intuition.

1.   Ask students to bring in materials which are cheap, durable, and safe (toys, household objects, etc.). With older students you may want to include hammers, nails, bolts, lumber, etc.

2.   Divide students into groups of five or six. By playing with the assembled objects, have students make discoveries about the sound potential of the objects they have brought in. Each group is to record their discoveries.

3.   Using the objects available to their group, students are to design a device that makes sound. Encourage students to use a variety of objects in as many different ways as possible. The important thing during this noisy period of play is to explore the rich realm of possibilities before arriving at one solution.

11. Create a Sound Garden

Ask students to imagine things they could hear in a garden, birds, the sound of the wind, leaves, human noises, etc. Discuss various ways sound could be generated in a garden, through wind, by walking, or sprinklers going, for example. Next, have students in small groups brainstorm ideas for a sound garden. Encourage creativity, fun ideas and original inventions.

Suggest inexpensive things that will hold up outdoors and will be safe for other children to play with (things that make sounds when walked on, when touched, etc.). Have groups draw up a design for their planned construction. Then bring ideas and items from home to contribute to the project. In their group, plan and construct your sound garden based on the items collected. Designs may have to be altered as the groups progress and ideas are adjusted to fit the materials and needs of construction. Teams must determine the best way to display their sound structures so that they will be accessible to others, function well, and create the best visual display in the garden.

12. Active Research: Exploring Pollution in the Earth's Spheres

Pollution is defined as an undesirable change in the properties of the lithosphere, hydrosphere, atmosphere or ecosphere that can have deleterious effects on humans and other organisms. A part of the task for student teams is to decide what an undesirable change is, or what is undesirable to them.

Tell the teams they are going to classify pollution in their neighborhood and city. The classification will be based on their senses and the different spheres of the earth: lithosphere (earth's crust), hydrosphere (earth's water), atmosphere (earth's gas), and ecosphere (the spheres in which life is formed). Give each group an observation sheet or have them design one that shows examples of pollution for a week:

OBSERVATIONS OF POLLUTION AND EARTH SPHERES

SENSES	LITOSPHERE	HYDROSPHERE	ATMOSPHERE	ECOSPHERE
sight				
touch				
hearing				
taste				
smell				

Figure 12.

Student teams are to record the types of pollution observed in the different earth's spheres. After a week of data gathering, discuss the groups' observations with the class. Teams may not have completed all the boxes of information. Discuss why this occurred. Also discuss discrepancies in groups' data and the reasons for this. Ask the class to identify the source of pollution and predict what might happen if the pollution continued. Have the groups figure out visual presentations of their data (slides, video, charts, graphs, newspaper story and illustrations, etc.). Class projects like these are frequently of interest to community organizations and news media.

13. Using Video Segments To Teach

Tape short segments from science and technology programs which deal with issues and concepts in your curriculum. Excerpts from science programs like NOVA, Wild Kingdom, Science and Technology Week, 3-2-1 Contact, or even the Weather Channel and the evening news offer a wealth of material. Design short projects based on these segments. An endangered species mural, a chart of weather patterns for the country, a computer newsletter, an audiotaped radio news release, etc. Student teams are great at coming up with their own projects, especially once you've sparked their interest on a topic.

14. Using the Newspaper To Teach About Math, Science and Technology

Major newspapers, like *The New York Times* and *The Washington Post* have weekly science and technology sections. Select a list of significant terms from the lead stories, pass out the papers or photocopies of the articles, and have students construct science fiction stories with the words and ideas from the feature science news page.

15. Graphing with Young Children

Instruct students to bring their favorite stuffed bear to school. As a class, sort the bears in various ways, size, color, type, etc. Graph the results with the class. Have pairs of students sort the bears in another way and paste paper counters or stickers on paper to make their own personalized graphs.

16. Estimate and Compare (K-1)

Place a similar group of objects in color-coded containers for each group in amounts of 7, 8, 10, etc. Pass out recording sheets divided into partitions with the color of the container in each box. Have young students examine the containers in their group, estimate how many objects are present, and write their guess next to the color on the sheet. Next, have the group count the objects and write the number counted next to the first number. Instruct the group to circle the greater amount. Then write a number sentence using the greather than sign (>). Switch cans or move to the next group station and repeat the process. A variety of objects (small plastic cats, marbles, paper clips, colored shells, etc.) add interest and are real motivators.

17. Simple Addition and Subtraction

Use manipulatives and have student teams paste counters beside the numbers. Some students need to see the whole pattern, so have them place counters where the answer will go.

18. Several New Visual Computer Programs

For secondary students we found that the computer program *Mathematica*, by Stephen Wolfram, was an excellent way to solve equations in algebra, geometry, and calculus with two-and three-dimensional illustrations on the video screen. Using this program pairs of students can manipulate three-dimensional plots of complex physical systems and visually manipulate complex formulas. This program can also simulate solutions for individual equations and visually manipulate concerns in theoretical math equations. There is a Macintosh, Sun Microsystems, and IBM version. And Steve Job's next machine comes with a free copy.

Logo Writer was initially designed as an integrated learning environment for the middle grades. Now there is a LogoWriter Primary, *Lego TC Logo* (hands-on toys for linking science, math and robotics). Logo Systems Inc., Boston, MA.

19. Using Logo Programming

Seymour Papert developed the Logo language to teach geometric concepts. He believes students can learn mathematical relationships more efficiently if they can project themselves into the world of mathematics. Students who can program a computer to draw a square or circle must understand the nature of a square or circle well enough to "teach" the computer. Using a logo program, such as "LogoWriter," even young student teams can develop short procedures and program the computer. Here are a few sample procedures using "LogoWriter."

```
To red square:
setc 3
repeat 4[fd 40 rt 90]
end
To yellow rectangle:
setc 4
repeat 2[fd 40 rt 90 fd 80 rt 90]
wait 60 cg
end
```

20. Arctic Survival Exercise

This exercise is adapted from survival experts and is presented as a problem-solving scenario for the group.

Your small plane carrying five passengers was forced to crash land in an isolated region in the Canadian north country, killing the pilot and damaging the aircraft beyond use. It is mid January and the temperature is −30 degrees Fahrenheit. The last reading taken by the pilot puts you in a position about twenty miles from the nearest town. Your small party was able to salvage the following articles from the plane:

- ball of steelwool
- compass
- hatchet
- plastic sectional air map
- can of shortening
- 20 × 20 foot piece of
  heavy canvas

- five newspapers
- loaded .45 caliber pistol
- cigarette lighter (without fluid)
- large chocolate bars
- quart of 100 proof whiskey
- extra shirt and pants
  per person

As a team you must decide on a plan for survival. Then rank order the items listed above in terms of priority for your survival plan. Number 1 indicates highest priority, 12 the lowest. When finished, check your responses with those of the survival experts.

Student break into teams to discuss and rank the items. They are instructed to base their plan rankings on team consensus. When disputes occur, strategies of compromise and group discussion towards agreement are to be used, rather than a simple point averaging system. When groups finish, compare the groups' responses with the whole class and with the experts.

Expert's Survival Plan

To survive, the team must plan to stay at the site. Most rescue attempts are made within 24 to 48 hours. Any attempt to walk out would almost certainly doom the team to death. The most pressing needs of the survivors are staying calm, warmth and shelter. Once the survivors have found ways to keep warm, their immediate problem is to attract the attention of the search parties. All of the items the group has salvaged will be assessed for their value in meeting these priorities.

Answer Key Experts ranking and explanations

1. **Cigarette lighter (without fluid)**

The greatest danger is exposure from the cold. The greatest need is for warmth. The second greatest need is for a signaling device. Building a fire should be the first priority. The cigarette lighter even without fuel will produce sparks to start a fire.

2. **Ball of steel wool**

Steel wool provides a means of catching the sparks made by the cigarette lighter. Steel wool, even if a little wool, provides the best substance for catching sparks and supporting a flame.

3. **Extra shirt and pants for each survivor**

Besides adding warmth to the body, these versatile items can be used for shelter, signaling, bedding, bandages, string, and tinder for fires.

4. **Can of shortening**

Both the can and its contents have many uses. Mirror-like signaling devices can be made from the lid. After shining the lid with steel wool it can be used as a sun reflector. A simple mirror can generate five to seven million candle power. The reflected beam can be seen beyond the horizon. Getting on a high point and signaling would greatly enhance the chances of rescue within 24 hours. Other uses: shortening can be rubbed on exposed areas for protection against the cold or eaten in small amounts. When melted it is useful for starting fires. When soaked into cloth it also will produce an effective candlewick. The can also has many uses like melting snow for drinking.

5. **20 × 20 foot heavy canvas**

Canvas can be used as shelter from wind and snow. It also makes a good signaling device.

6. **Hatchet**

Its many uses include: chopping wood, clearing the campsite, cutting boughs for ground insulation, and constructing a frame for a shelter.

7.   Five large chocolate bars

Chocolate provides a quick energy source without making digestive demands on the system.

8.   Newspapers

Newspapers can be used for starting fires or used as an insulator when rolled and placed under clothing. They provide dead air space for protection from the cold. Other uses: reading recreation, spread for signaling purposes, rolled into a cone for voice signaling.

9.   Loaded .45 caliber pistol

The pistol provides a sound signaling device (3 shots is an international distress signal). This is especially important as survivors get weaker and unable to make loud responses. The butt can be used as a hammer. The shell powder is useful in starting fires.

Unfortunately, the pistol's disadvantages counterbalance its advantages. Anger, lapses of rationality, and frustration make a lethal weapon dangerous under these circumstances. Too much energy would be expended by individuals to hunt with this weapon. It would take a skilled marksman to kill an animal and too much energy would be used in transporting it.

10.   Quart of 100-proof whiskey

The only productive uses are its use in fire building and as a fuel. Alcohol takes on the temperature it is exposed to. Drinking it at minus 20 degrees poses a serious danger to the mouth. (Drinking it warmer causes dehydration.) Alcohol contributes to a rapid loss of body heat.

11.   Compass

This is a dangerous item because it may encourage some survivors to attempt to walk to the nearest town. The glass may be used as a sun signal reflector, but it is the least effective of the potential devices.

12.   Sectional air map

This item is dangerous because it will encourage members to walk to the nearest town, thereby condemning them to almost certain death.

21. Group Problem Solving With Mathematical Patterns

This cooperative logic problem works best for groups of four or six students. Cut apart the set of clue cards (below). Make one set of cards for each group. Pass out a set of colored blocks to each table (pattern blocks or cubes work well). Choose a group leader to pass out the cards, one for each person in the group. Each student may look at their own clue or clues but are instructed not to show their card to anyone else. Students work together to solve the problem. Students may talk while they are working but are not to reveal the information on their card except through actions and negotiations.

Clue Cards:

There are six blocks in a tower. The tower is six blocks high. There is a yellow block on top.

The red block is above the green block.

One of the yellow blocks is above the green block; the other is below it.

Each of the blue blocks shares a face with the green block.

There are two yellows, two blues, one green, and one red in the set of blocks.

No two blocks of the same color touch each other.

REFERENCES

Arbib, M.: *Brains, Machines and Mathematics.* New York, Springer-Verlag, 1987.

Aronowitz, S.: *Science As Power: Discourse and Ideology in Modern Society.* Minneapolis, University of Minnesota Press.

Brown, H.: *The Wisdom of Science: Its Relevance to Culture and Religion.* New York, Cambridge University Press, 1986.

Bruner, J., & Haste, H.: *Making Sense.* New York, Routledge, 1987.

Burns, M.: *The Good Times Math Event Book.* Oak Lawn, IL, Creative Publications, 1977.

Bybee, R.: Global problems and science education policy. *1984 NSTA Yearbook.* Washington, D.C., National Science Teachers Association, 1984.

Carey, N., Mittman, B., & Darling-Hammand, L.: *Recruiting Mathematics and Science Teachers Through Nontraditional Programs: A Survey.* Santa Monica, CA, Rand Corporation, 1989.

Carson, J., & Bostick, R.: *Math Instruction Using Media and Modality Strengths.* Springfield, Charles C Thomas, 1988.

Champagne, A., and Klopfer, L.: Research in Science Education: The Cognitive Perspective. *Research Within Reach: Science Education,* 1988.

Charleston, WV, Research and Development Interpretation Service, 1984. Education Progress Service Inc.: *Guide to Free Computer Material* (videotapes, discs, etc.), Randolph, Wisconsin 414-326-3126.

Chickering, A. *Experience and Learning.* Rochelle, NY, Change Magazine Press, 1977.

Clark, C., Carter, B., & Sternberg, B.: *Math In Stride.* Menlo Park, CA, Addison-Wesley, 1988.

Forman, G., & Pufall, P. (Eds.): *Constructivism in the Computer Age.* Hillsdale, NJ, Lawrence Erlbaum, 1988.

Garofalo, J. "Metacognition and School Mathematics," *The Arithmetic Teacher. 34*(3), 22–23.

Gleick, J.: *Chaos.* New York, Viking, 1987.

Harms, N., & Yager, R. (1981). *What Research Says To the Science Teacher, 3.* Washington, D.C.: NSTA, 471-14776, 1981.

Hughes, M.: *Children and Number: Difficulties In Learning Mathematics.* New York, Blackwell, 1986.

Johnson, G. (1986). *Machinery of the Mind.* New York: Times Books, Random House Publishing.

Kaseverg, A., Kreinberg, N., & Downie, D.: *Use EQUALS to Promote the Participation of Women In Mathematics.* Berkeley, CA, Lawrence Hall of Science, 1980.

Kitcher, P. (1983). *The Nature of Mathematical Knowledge.* New York, Oxford University Press.

Koonin, S. (1986). *Computational Physics.* Menlo Park, CA, Benjamin/Cummings Publishing.

Langbort, C., & Thompson, V.: *Building Success in Math.* Belmont, CA, Wadsworth Publishing, 1985.

Meyer, C., & Sallee, T.: *Make It Simpler: A Practical Guide to Problem Solving in Mathematics.* Menlo Park, CA, Addison-Wesley, 1983.

Miller, A. (1986). *Imagery In Scientific Thought.* Cambridge, MA, The MIT Press.

National Science Teachers Association: *NSTA Position Statement On School Science Education for the 1980s.* Washington, D.C.: NSTA, 1982.

Noble, G.: *Children In Front of the Small Screen.* London: Constable, 1975.

Nelson, J.: *The Perfect Machine: TV in the Nuclear Age.* Canada, Between the Lines, Inc., 1988.

Paul, R., Binker, K., Jensen, K., & Kreklau, H.: *Critical Thinking Handbook.* Rohnert Park, CA, Sonoma State University, 1989.

Rouse, J.: *Knowledge and Power: Toward a Political Philosophy of Science.* Ithaca, Cornell University Press, 1988.

Rucker, R. (1987). *Mind Tools.* Boston, MA, Houghton Mifflin Co.

Shoenfeld, A. (1985). *Mathematical Problem Solving.* Orlando, FL, Academic Press, Inc.

Shulman, J., & Colbert, J.: *The Mentor Teacher Casebook.* ERIC Clearinghouse on Educational Management, 1987.

Silver, E. (1985). "Research On Teaching Mathematical Problem Solving: Some Underrepresented Themes." In *Teaching and Learning Mathematical Problem Solving: Multiple Research Perspectives.* E. Silver (Ed.). Hillsdale, NJ, Lawrence Erlbaum Associates.

Slavin, R.: *School and Classroom Organization.* Hillsdale, NJ, Erlbaum 1989.

Stake, R., & Easley, J. et al.: *Case Studies in Science Education.* Urbana, IL, University of Illinois, 1978.

Stenmark, J., Thompson, V., & Cossey, R.: *Family Math.* Palo Alto, CA, Dale Seymour Press, 1986.

Tobin, K., & Fraser, B.: Case studies of exemplary science and mathematics teaching. *School Science and Mathematics,* 89(4), 1989.

Weiss, I.: *Report of the 1977 National Survey of Science Education.* Washington, D.C.: U.S. Government Printing Office, 1977.

6

COOPERATIVE LEARNING, MAINSTREAMING AND EXCEPTIONAL STUDENTS: ACCOMMODATING STUDENTS WITH SPECIAL NEEDS IN REGULAR CLASSROOMS

Making a space for diversity in the presence of others involves caring and community. Going beyond labels, we need a commitment to tap the multiple realities of human experience. . . . Such an education for freedom takes into account our political and social realities as well as the human condition itself.

—Maxine Greene

The percentage of students with special needs has remained at about 11 percent of the school population. There has, however, been a substantial increase in students identified as "learning disabled" (LD). Learning disabled students now make up nearly 45 percent of all special education students. Unless they have a learning disability, gifted and talented youth are usually not included in this specialized count because they spend the bulk of their time in regular classrooms. A recent Gallop poll showed nearly half the nation willing to spend more money for children with learning problems (than for normal progress children). But, although they are recognized to have special needs, only 25 percent would spend more money for gifted and talented children. Also, gifted programs do not get the same level of popular support as those students who are having trouble learning. This chapter will discuss cooperative learning in the context of a broad range of exceptional children—the academically handicapped and the academically talented students.

Education of All Handicapped Children Act (PL 94-142) has been in effect for over a decade now and continues to receive wide support from teachers, parents and legislators.[1] Among other things, it gives children with any type of disability the right to learn in the "least restrictive environment." This means working, at least part of the time, with mixed-

---

1. Cummings, R. W., & Cleborne, D. M.: *Parenting the Learning Disabled: A Realistic Approach.* Springfield, IL, Charles C Thomas, 1985.

ability groups of "regular" children in "regular" classrooms. It also involves developing and adhering to an individualized education plan (IEP) which specifies how much time is to be spent in special and regular settings.[2]

Students with special needs can also profit from being able to control their own thinking, attitude, and attention span. In the same vein, they can profit from reasoned thought processes that focus on what to believe or do (critical thinking) and being able to form new combinations of original ideas (creative thinking). The special education and the regular classroom teacher can work together to provide the framework needed to help students with special needs make the necessary connection with peers.

In 1986, the U.S. Office of Education suggested that since students with special needs profited from being in regular classes, there was little or no need for special education. Students with special needs could simply be placed in regular classes. The Regular Education Initiative (REI) failed, in part, because it involved cutting support for special needs *and* students across the board. The basic intent wasn't to improve services but to save money. Mainstreaming was one thing, unassisted regular classroom increases in student populations with severe learning needs is quite another. The research suggests that exceptional students have more to lose than their peers if deficits are left unattended.[3]

This chapter, with Vern Simula and Aliceon Stillman, sets out to find ways to accommodate handicapped students within "regular" "mainstreamed" classrooms. Teachers and parents alike have long searched for ways for all exceptional students to receive an "appropriate" education in the most appropriate learning environment. Labeling and separating children has been harmful. And so has shunting students with disabilities off into a large class with a regular classroom teacher who lacks the training or support to give these students the attention they need. The best approach lies someplace in between. The problem is *where.*

Connecting Special Needs Students To the Curriculum

Educators generally agree that each child has the basic human right to be "successful" in school: that is, each child has the right to enjoy

2. Sternberg, L., Taylor, R., & Schilt, J. *So You're Not A Special Educator.* Springfield, IL, Charles C Thomas, 1986.

3. Nevin, A., Thousand, J., & Fox, W.: Promising practices: An inservice training model integrating severely handicapped learners. *Teacher Education and Special Education,* 10(1), 1987.

learning, to undertake learning tasks that challenge but that do not overwhelm, to achieve, to know and sense that they can learn, to enjoy being in school and to thrive and to grow from the schooling experience.

The search for effective techniques for mainstreaming or integrating students who have various types of handicaps has not been an easy one, nor has it been a sufficiently successful search. "Children with disabilities . . . are still often rejected from the 'mainstream' programs and whisked off to special places for their education. Thus, rejection processes still operate within many schools. . . . "[4] School life is group life, and part of what schools are about is teaching students how to live effectively in diverse groups. Yet, there is a troubling dissonance between our stated values and our revealing practices. What are the obstacles that block teachers from fully and genuinely integrating students with disabilities into their classrooms?

The phrase "to accommodate the needs of students with disabilities into our classrooms" implicitly suggests a belief that the primary or original placement of the student with a disability is or should be somewhere other than in the regular classroom. The phrase additionally implies that teachers are being morally and legally obligated to now bring those students into their classrooms and to accommodate their learning needs. With higher average classroom scores on standardized tests being a prime determinant of teaching "success," it is little wonder that classroom teachers fear an influx of special students who don't do well on these assessment instruments.

Our current model of schooling gradually established the position that regular classroom teachers did not need to assume primary responsibility for student with disabilities. Special education, which developed over the last century, was thought to provide more suitable programs for children and young adults who could not succeed in the regular program as the regular program was structured. From this beginning, special education grew to become a subsystem of regular education—and later a parallel system to regular education.[5] Now, as we enter the second decade of PL 94-142, it is important for schools to try new things and help regular educators broaden their repertoire of methods so that they can reach a broader group of students.

---

4. Reynolds, Maynard. "Past, Present, and Future of School Integration." In *Minnesota UAP Impact,* Volume 1 (2), Winter 1988. A report of the Minnesota University Affiliate Program on Developmental Disabilities. Minneapolis, Minn.: University of Minnesota.

5. Flynn, George and Kowalczyk-McPhee, Bernie. "A School System in Transition." (unpublished manuscript).

Figure 13.

School grouping and segregation policies are sometimes the real cause of making a child being perceived as different, rather than the child's disability per se. When children don't adjust well to the school curriculum (and many don't), they are frequently labeled "handicapped" and separated from their peers. Here we look at avenues for making changes in the schooling process so that children can be grouped with their peers as much as possible. It recognizes that part of the time some exceptional students may need special settings. And, most importantly, quality experiences must occur across educational settings.

Cooperative learning with·special needs students is not simply a technique that a teacher can just select and adopt in order to "accommodate" a student with a disability within the regular classroom in order to satisfy the "least restrictive environment" requirement of the IEP. Making significant change in the classroom process is going to require that teachers undergo changes in the ways that they teach and in the ways they view students. This means creating comfortable, yet challenging, learning environments rich in diversity. The goal is cooperation among all types of learners. In mixed-ability groups the emphasis must be on proficiency rather than age or grade level as a basis for student progress.

Cooperative learning is a "total class" approach that lends itself to mainstreaming.[6] It requires everyone to think, learn, and teach. Within a cooperative learning classroom, there will be many and varied "differences" among students. Every student will possess differences that will lend themselves to enriching learning for all students. Sometimes these "differences" may constitute a conventionally defined "disability," sometimes it simply means the inability to do a certain life or school-related task. And sometimes it means, as with the academically talented, being capable of work well beyond the norm. Within the cooperative learning classroom, such exceptionality need not constitute a handicap.

Strategies for Change

Active collaboration requires a depth of planning, a redefinition of planning, testing, and classroom management. Perhaps most significantly, cooperative learning values differences of abilities, talents, skills and background knowledge. Within a cooperative learning classroom, conventionally defined "disabilities" fade into the heterogeneity of expected and anticipated differences among all students. "Disabilities" and "differences" come to constitute part of the fabric of diversity that is celebrated and cherished within the cooperative learning classroom. In such an educational climate, no individual is singled out as being different. No one student presents a challenge to the teacher as to how to accommodate a student with special needs.

In a cooperative learning classroom, no student needs to be stereotyped by others when they realize that there are many and varied "differences" among students. It is easier for the student with special needs to fit in. For some pupils "differences" may in fact constitute a "disability," defined as the inability to do a certain life or school-related task. Such a difference, however, need not constitute a handicap, as cooperative learning is a joint enterprise. Some may have a disability or

---

6. Wang, M. C., & Birch, J. W. (Eds.). *Handbook of Special Education Research and Practice*, Vol. 1. London: Pergamon Press, 1987.

special talent, but all have information and skills to contribute to the learning of others.

The central question is, How do individual classroom teachers, already overwhelmed with tasks, find ways to adapt techniques and modify approaches to successfully accommodate one or more students with a disability within their classrooms? After all, the stress of responding to the needs of a typical classroom is demanding enough. The problem is more than adapting techniques or modifying current approaches and getting the support of special education specialists. It involves rethinking— seeking different approaches for teaching all students that lend themselves to accommodating unique human qualities.

Research on Collaborative Learning and Mainstreamed Students

Mainstreaming physically or mentally handicapped students with their normal-progress peers presents enormous practical problems for classroom teachers and often leads to social rejection for special needs students. Cooperative learning methods have been so successful in reducing ethnic barriers it seems appropriate to apply them to mainstreamed students.[7]

Research on cooperative learning with mainstreamed students has shown significant gains in academic achievement and self-esteem.[8] Cooperative learning also significantly reduced the degree of rejection encountered by these students and increased positive interaction and gained friendships.[9] Even emotionally disturbed students were more on task and better behaved than students not involved in collaborative groups.[10]

Perhaps most importantly, using cooperative learning methods in mainstreamed classrooms benefited all students in terms of academic achievement, self-esteem and positive interaction. Students reported being more accepted by their peers and enjoying the camaraderie of

7. Gerard, H. B., & Miller, N.: *School Desegregation: A Long Range Study.* New York, Plenum, 1975.

8. Madden, N. A., & Slavin, R. E. "Cooperative Learning and Social Acceptance of Mainstreamed Academically Handicapped Students." *Journal of Special Education,* 17, 1983, 171–82.

9. Slavin, R. E., Madden, N. E., & Leavy, M. B. "Effects of Team Assisted Individualization on the Mathematics Achievement of Academically Handicapped and Nonhandicapped Students." *Journal of Educational Psychology,* 76, 1984, 813–19.

10. Janke, R. "The Teams-Games-Tournament (TGT) Method and the Behavioral Adjustment and Academic Achievement of Emotionally Impaired Adolescents." Paper presented at annual convention of American Educational Research Association, Toronto, 1978.

working in small groups. Many reported feeling more comfortable working in teams and more successful in their approach to academic tasks.
Cooperative supportive experiences in school were found to help withdrawn children and those with antisocial attitudes outside of school.[11]

With such success why have many teachers been slow to respond? One
explanation for such resistance is that cooperative learning procedures
are different from the traditional competitive, stimulus-response model
of teaching and learning. There is a fear of not knowing how to act or
"behave" when relating to a cooperative learning setting. Additionally,
teachers have not been trained in how to organize a cooperative learning
"flow" of events and materials. For teachers to successfully link collaboration and mainstreaming they need models and the opportunity to experience cooperative teaching and learning in action. Familiarity with a
conceptual model makes vitalized cooperative groups in the classroom
easier.

New Assumptions, New Models, New Processes

As our society as a whole is now in the midst of a transition from an
industrial society to an "information-age" society, so is it that new conceptual models, new ways of thinking, are also emerging. Two of the central
features of the information-age society are "communication" and "net-
working." These two hallmarks suggest the basic paradigm for a new
model not only for industry but for education as well. There a many
intriguing assumptions suggested by the new communications/networking
model. These new assumptions will serve to "shake the foundations" of
much of what we have believed in the past to be important and essential
to the process of schooling. The following list suggests but a few:

1. Learning is an active, very social process. Many people need to be
   involved with others.
2. Learning is a very active mental process. The mind is always
   working, always learning. Critical and creative thinking skills
   help students generalize by adding information beyond what
   is given.
3. The prior experience of a student is an important ingredient of
   any learning situation.

---

11. Slavin, R. E. "A Student Team Approach To Teaching Adolescents with Special Emotional and
Behavioral Needs." *Psychology in the Schools,* 14 (1), 1977, 77–8.

4. The student must be a real active, self-initiating participant in the learning process.
5. Students need to verbalize their experiences and their new learnings on their own (language and conceptual) terms. Developing metaphors and analogies can assist with extending thinking and language.
6. Students are excellent teachers. They can teach each other. They can learn as much from their peers as from teachers.
7. The "things" to be learned are not really as compartmentalized as current curriculum fields may suggest. Everything is related and interrelated. Students need to discover these relationships. The relationships that students come up with may be different than the ones that teachers have because of differences in levels of past experiences and cognitive maturity.
8. Students are tremendously curious. They have a tremendous need to learn, to become competent.
9. Students enjoy and profit tremendously from working together and thereby learning together.
10. With proper development, students can become very responsible for managing their own learning opportunities.

All of these assumptions, coupled with a cooperative learning approach, will lead to much different styles of teaching for the teacher. Interaction and information flow are major characteristics of the teaching/learning style. The "richer" the interaction, the more productive the learning. As students and teachers undertake learning projects, they become joint ventures. Success (or grades) are not determined by who competitively achieves the highest score on a test. Rather, it is determined by how well the learning project is accomplished and how well the various members of the learning "team" have interacted and worked together.

The characteristics of cooperation, interaction and diversity are vital to the thinking and developmental needs of all students, but especially for the student with more severe motor, speech or learning problems. Exceptional students who are academically talented or gifted can also gain important understandings by being work partners and friends with a wide range of peers.

MOVING TO A COOPERATIVE
LEARNING CLASSROOM ENVIRONMENT

The leap from the familiar competitive, stimulus-response, production control model of schooling to a communication cooperative model can seem enormous. To consider a change of such magnitude can seem threatening and unnerving. How then can we make the transition and the emotional adjustments?

One way is to realize the similarities between how the teaching process is now organized and how it would be using cooperative learning strategies. There is considerable structure, motivation and individual freedom within cooperative learning. Trusting peers and valuing diverse contributions is central to developing a collaborative framework. Cooperative learning can be applied within any curriculum area as conventionally defined by existing curriculum guides or content area textbooks. Thus, a teacher can adapt this model quite easily without making drastic changes to the knowledge or skill objectives that are already specified for a course.[12] The textbook does not have to be thrown out but, rather, extended to include active learning procedures where student groups are involved in searching out information, clarifying and explaining concepts, working on cooperative projects, solving problems, "finding out—rather than filling in."

When they use cooperative learning strategies teachers stress the importance of experiential and world knowledge in learning. New material, information, knowledge, and skills, are explored, interpreted and extended on the basis of what the students already know. This integration is suggested by the recent development of the "whole language" approach to learning in the mainstreamed classroom. Whole language is a shorthand way of referring to a set of beliefs about curriculum, not just language arts curriculum, but about everything that goes on in classrooms.[13] In this approach, students read real literature rather than textbooks and relate reading to personal experiences. Cooperative learning lends itself to integrate this process across subject matter areas: social studies, science, mathematics, and the fine arts.

The whole language approach places heavy emphasis on the importance of the students' prior knowledge but extends this concept in two

---

12. Salvia, J., & Ysseldyke, J. *Assessment in Special and Remedial Education.* Houghton Mifflin, 1989.

13. Newman, Judith M. (Ed.). *Whole Language.* Portsmouth, New Hampshire: Heinemann, 1985.

important ways. One is that it is crucial for students to "create their own knowledge" by engaging in the learning process. In the whole language model, students are not passive recipients of information or skills. They are encouraged to actively "engage their worlds" in order to learn and "construct their own meanings" by expressing their ideas through talking, but especially through writing. Students engage topics and problems that have strong personal meaning to them.

The Central Role of the Teacher

There is general agreement that American schools don't have a choice about changing. Our educational systems need massive, system-wide restructuring and educators must be intimately involved in the effort. At the school site level there must be wider participation by all faculty in developing school policy. It's too late for tinkering around the edges. Teachers need time and incentives for becoming involved in taking on new responsibilities, planning, collaborating with peers and attending in-service programs to keep their skills at a high level. And new teachers need thorough orientation programs and mentors who are successful in the school environment where they are expected to teach. Consciously thinking about and affirming a new set of values means recognizing the importance of diversity, valuing students' prior knowledge, and actively engaging student groups in the learning process. Many educators are in the process of making the transition from the competitive/stimulus-response-production control model, where the teacher is somewhat of an external operator of the system, to a model of cooperation, where the teacher is a facilitator or academic choreographer.

When teachers have assimilated the cooperative learning paradigm as their principle teaching style and when student diversity is appreciated, students with learning disabilities will benefit along with everyone else.[14] In some cases, depending upon the severity of the disability, there will be a different set of teacher responsibilities. Yet, within the context of cooperative teaching and learning, the demands for integrating students with diverse needs are much more easily absorbed because of the nature of the teaching/learning process. As peers take responsibility for some of

14. Lerner, J.: *Learning Disabilities: Theories, Diagnosis, and Teaching Strategies.* Boston, Houghton Mifflin, 1989.

the teaching, the power of the teacher can be multiplied. When coopera-tive groups are used, it has proved beneficial to all.[15]

Collaboration With Colleagues

Inherent in the concept of the cooperative model is the notion of teacher-to-teacher collaboration. The interactive nature of the coopera-tive model itself enhances the possibility of working closely, collaboratively, with many other teachers and support professionals. In some schools this may mean a revamping of traditional departmental arrangements to facilitate interdisciplinary coordination.

Teachers with strengths in social science topics may find themselves planning and working with teachers whose strengths are in music or science or language. Similarly, classroom teachers may find themselves working jointly with special education teachers. Making sure that teachers have collaborative opportunities is central to involving them in a larger role such as shaping their profession or changing school organizational patterns. As a team, teachers can plan and teach together to meet the equal access needs of students. They can also jointly plan enrichment activities for those exceptional students who are academically talented — breaking down the barriers known as "regular" education and "special" education. This collaboration between professionals allows the regular classroom teacher to broaden their teaching techniques — and reach a wider range of students.

A Collaborative Model for Students and Teachers

Teaching is the only profession where what you do
evaporates almost as soon as it's done.
It's just gone. It's fleeting memories.
— Lee Shulman

Collaboration models place exceptional students into normal-progress classrooms where a team made up of regular classroom teachers and special educators can better serve all students. The regular classroom teacher structures the physical environment and provides broad educa-tional goals and curricula; the special education teachers adapts methods

---

15. Mercer, C.D., & Mercer, A. R.: *Teaching Students With Learning Problems.* Columbus, OH, Merrill, 1985.

and materials to meet the needs of low-achieving learning disabled and other students with special needs.[16]

The research suggests that a wide range of students in cooperative learning situations (in a mainstreamed setting) had significantly higher achievement gains in reading and mathematics. They also felt more satisfied and perceived their work as less difficult. In addition, teachers who worked with colleagues on collaborative projects were very positive about the support system which developed and the benefits to learning. They reported the process added to students' and teachers' enjoyment of learning and improved the educational experiences of both.[17]

Computers As Prosthetic Devices and Learning Tools

For students with more severe learning handicaps the computer can function as an adaptive device to help them reenter the school community. Increased access to the curriculum is gained by using the technology to break down concepts of abstraction and time. Computers can also provide graphic representations of abstract ideas in ways that are more accessible to mildly handicapped students. And they can help a student with poor handwriting, for example, eliminate that difficulty (with a word processing program) and help simplify the revision process.

By connecting software with cooperative learning children can jointly write a story, travel through time, or interact visually with chemical elements. This means that as the technology advances there will probably be an increase in the amount of time that special education students can spend in regular classrooms. Computing can also help put this time to more integrated use by increasing the socialization among diverse student groups. In part, this is because what's on the computer screen is a great equalizer. What's viewed on the monitor is often seen as something of a public document—increasing contact with peer collaborators.

Computers can help break down the barriers between students as they explore the intellectual landscape and teach one another. As a consequence, the technology is challenging some of the preconceived

---

16. Bartoli, J., & Botel, M.: *Reading/Learning Disability: An Ecological Approach.* New York, Teachers College Press, 1989.

17. Carlson, H., Ellison, D., & Dietrich, J.: *Servicing Low Achieving Pupils and Pupils with Learning Disabilities: A Comparison of Two Approaches.* ERIC ED 283 341.

notions about disabilities as it helps special needs students keep up in regular classrooms.[18]

Mildly handicapped students make up the bulk of the students who received special education services. Here, the computers have proven their value by helping such students at traditional academic tasks. In a classroom where few students know how to use a new piece of software, we have found it useful to teach special needs students first so they may explain it to others. They are then seen as having an important skill that classmates need help with.

The Center for Applied Special Technology (Peabody, MA) and the National Special Education Alliance (Cupertino, CA) provide suggestions for increasing the use of computer hardware and software for students with disabilities. The special education technology lab at the University of Connecticut even publishes a software evaluation bulletin for educators that can help in connecting computer software to special needs students in regular classroom groups.

MEETING SPECIAL NEEDS OF GIFTED, ACADEMICALLY TALENTED STUDENTS IN REGULAR CLASSROOMS

Without spotlighting them there are unique collaborative learning possibilities that exist when there are a few academically talented or gifted students in a class. Under the right conditions they can advance socially, develop intellectually and make a special contribution to the regular classroom. The research evidence from related fields is overwhelming: students of all ability levels learn more and have better attitudes (towards others) when they work together as a group.[19] Cooperative learning activities can help the gifted avoid boredom—while assisting regular students.

By providing the right kind of learning activities the classroom teacher can build on the power of collaborative peer learning to help students actively (and democratically) work together to develop ideas and solve problems.[20] As regular and gifted students talk and work together the

18. Kelly, R.: Computers and sensory impaired individuals. In J. D. Lindsey (Ed.), *Computers and Exceptional Individuals.* Columbus, OH, Merrill, 1985.

19. Wang, M.C., & Walberg, H. J. (Eds). *Adapting Instruction To Individual Differences.* Berkeley, CA, McCutchan, 1985.

20. Slavin, R. "Ability Grouping and Student Achievement in Elementary Schools; A Best Evidence Synthesis. *Review of Educational Research,* 57, 1987, 293–336.

three aspects of intelligence

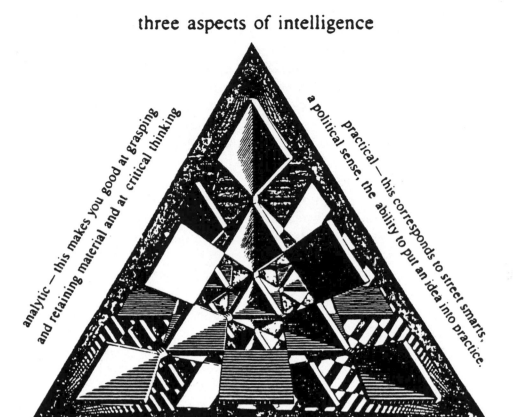

analytic — this makes you good at grasping and retaining material and at critical thinking

practical — this corresponds to street smarts, a political sense, the ability to put an idea into practice.

synthetic — the usual name for this is creativity; it
gives you the power to come up with new ideas, new solutions to a problem

Figure 14.

teacher facilitates learning by maintaining a good learning scene, monitoring group progress and demonstrating the unique power of peer collaboration.

Concepts for Regular Classroom Teachers To Consider

Learning style characteristics of gifted children are something regular classroom teachers need to be aware of. Once their needs and leadership qualities are understood by the regular classroom teacher, the teacher can develop organizational patterns and make use of collaborative learning strategies that benefit everyone. Keeping gifted Jane from getting bored can also help not so academically talented Johnny learn. By collaboration with other students, the gifted student can help everyone move forward while preparing for the leadership roles that are so important to our society's future.

Problem-finding is one of the most important skills for the gifted learner. The ability to look at specific events and decide which ones are worthy of further analysis is a socially useful skill that we squander at our own risk. Working together, all children in the classroom can move from absorbing facts to thinking of solutions to the problems and, ultimately, to deciding which problems are most urgent to solve.

A gifted program component cannot be overlooked, as there are many high-quality models on which to build (the district's gifted coordinator can help here). The difference such programs make to gifted students should not be underestimated. In studies of gifted high school graduates, for example, it was found that gifted programs do make a difference in achievement and accomplishments and attitudes of students enrolled. High grade point averages, test scores, honors, self-concepts, and vocational goals were demonstrated among students in special programs for the academically talented.

A major difference between high-achieving and low-achieving gifted students is the stimulation provided from the home. There is no substitute for parental involvement. It is important for the parent—as well as the teacher and child—to realize that there are at least a few other gifted students around. When parents help with coping strategies and give encouragement, students are more involved and complete higher-quality products.

Integrating All Students Into an Active Group Process

A carefully balanced combination of direct instruction, self-monitoring and active group work helps meet diverse special needs. With some students basic skills must be developed before higher order skills can be taught. These students need a highly structured skill work based program, part of the day, so that they can participate in open-ended group work projects. This means a careful balance between needs and interests.

Special education programs in many communities are partial send-out type classes. Pull-out programs can result in fragmentation where neither the special or regular teacher is fully responsible. The resource room can also give children the best of both worlds if the quality of learning is high. Resource room instruction is most successful when it avoids having children spend a large amount of time working independently at their seats.[21]

When working in cooperative groups on the basis of equity-across-ability levels becomes a natural part of regular classroom life, teachers have a more constant opportunity to increase everyone's rate of academic success while making learning more stimulating for everyone. Regular classroom teachers report little difficulty devising questions and classroom situations in which mainstreamed and regular students, in mixed-ability groups, confirm and disconfirm one another's observations on the basis of solid reasoning.

Exceptional students, including the gifted, are different because they have abilities that deviate from regular expectations. The research suggests when these students receive mainstream and differentiated educational possibilities they will make a better contribution to themselves and to society.[22] However, it does take more than deciding that cooperative learning for students with vastly different abilities makes sense in an increasingly interdependent society. Teachers need to be aware of how they can help students across ability levels develop collaborative learning skills.

The needs of mainstreamed students can be met most effectively when there are opportunities for frequent contact between regular and special education teachers. Once students see that peers look collectively to all members of the group for advice on various processes and products, collaboration flourishes. With practice, all teachers become more adept at forming groups, setting tasks and monitoring progress.

Increasing the social interaction of exceptional students is a challenge to teachers who are usually charged with covering a certain amount of material in a particular way. But it's worth the effort. The notion that "none of us is as smart as all of us" is true. Collaboration between students with special needs and regular students can help both groups learn by assimilating and generating knowledge through group interaction and individual accountability.

---

21. Haynes, M., & Jenkins, R. "Reading Instruction in Special Education Resource Rooms." *American Educational Research Journal,* 23(2), 1986, 161–190.

22. Gersten, R., Walker, H., & Darch, C. "Relationship Between Teachers' Effectiveness and Their Tolerance for Handicapped Students." *Exceptional Children,* 54(5), 1988, 433–438.

SAMPLE ACTIVITIES

1. Collage Photo Art

Students at all levels can become producers as well as consumers of art. We used a videotape of David Hockney's work from *Art in America.* Hockney, one of today's important artists, spoke (on the videotape) about his work and explained his technique. Students then used cameras to explore Hockney's photo collage technique in their own environment. Student groups can arrange several sets of their photos differently — telling unique stories with different compositions of the same pictures. Teachers do need to preview any videos before they are used in the classroom, because some parts may not be appropriate for elementary school children. Teachers can also select particular elements and transfer them from one VCR to another so that only the useful segments are present on the tape used in class.

2. Examine Similarities in Folk Lore and Literature

Have student groups explore myths, folktales, legends and fairytales to look for similarities and differences between people, times and cultures. Construct a group list, concept map, collage, visual image, or writing that shows these group findings.

3. Make Use of Biographies

Biographies can provide information about values, motives and accomplishments — acting as role models for students. Historical fiction enables students to gain an appreciation of various authors' works and to show literature is not written in isolation. Particular themes such as those in Faust and Prometheus serve as discussions for major themes of mankind.

4. Focus on Inquiry Skills

Emphasis on inquiry skills and the processes of science has made a significant difference on student knowledge, skills mastery and attitudes. Problem solving and critical thinking can be taught throughout the curriculum in which the teacher continues to be a learner. Helping regular/special students develop an understanding of inquiry (finding out though hypothesis testing, data collection, reporting, generalizing conclusions, communicating results) is an important intellectual tool which will prove to be a lasting contribution as they move toward lifelong learning.

5. Present the Historical View

To keep children from concluding that everything worth knowing has already been discovered. Present an historical view in such subjects as mathematics, astronomy, literature, art, etc.

6. Connect Areas of Learning with Practical Applications

Concepts in subject areas make sense to students when they are applied to real situations. Applications of mathematical concepts, such as probability, are made in insurance, biology, physics, weather forecasting, psychology, social science, medical research, as well as many sports and recreational activities. Encourage students to explore areas where concepts like these are used. Using resources such as newspapers, outside experts, friends, adults, books, TV programs, etc., construct a group list of all the ways a concept, like probability, is used. Students may give examples and supply resources or references, act out probability scenarios, etc.

7. Create Writing Partnerships

A common collaborative learning strategy is to divide the partnership into a "thinker" and a "writer." One partner reads a short concept or question out loud and tells what he or she thinks the answer should be. The writer writes it down if they agree. If not, they try to convince the "thinker" that there is a better answer. If agreement cannot be reached, they write two answers and initial one.

8. Brainstorm

In pairs, have students brainstorm a topic, e.g. list as many things as you can think of that move, things that are deep, sharp, white or soft. You may wish to set a three- or five-minute time limit.

9. Generate Ideas: Convergent Thinking

Take a situation in current events or from literature and have students in small groups generate ideas for ten minutes with judgment deferred. Then take ten minutes to have the group evaluate their ideas. Instruct group members to make a list of their five best and five silliest ideas to share with the class. (Explain that the most unlikely ideas frequently result in the best solutions.)

Example. Take the situation from the Daniel Defoe book *Robinson Crusoe* —put yourself in his situation. Washed ashore on a desert island with nothing but a large belt and belt buckle. How can these tools be used to survive? (A) ten minutes—generate as many ideas as possible, (B) ten minutes—to evaluate, (C) Bring the best and funniest back to the whole class.

Group Evaluation Activity

Count fluency scores by giving one point for a common response and three points for a creative one. Have each group choose one creative response and expand on that idea by writing a paragraph. Share paragraphs and include them in a class book for others to read. These activities develop students' ability to think divergently, a skill which many academically gifted students do not have.

Suggestions From the Research

Active learning activities can promote thinking and cooperation among all students. The research on effective instruction suggests a number of points of agreement:

Good instructional practice:

1. respects different interests, abilities, and learning styles.
2. uses active learning techniques to relate what's being learned to a student's personal environment.
3. develops collaboration and reciprocation.
4. communicates high expectations.[23]

Involving gifted, regular and handicapped students in cooperative work lessons or classroom projects can help develop reflective thinking

---

23. Stiggins, R., Rubel, E., & Edys, Q.: *Measuring Thinking Skills in the Classroom.* Washington, D.C., National Education Association, 1988.

and active decision-making skills across all student ability levels. Developing high-interest strategies that are based on fluency, flexibility, originality and elaboration in creative thinking profits everyone.

REFERENCES

Allen, W. H., & Van Sichle, R. L. "Learning teams and low achievers." *Social Education*, 1984.

Ballard, M. "Improving the Social Status of Mainstreamed Retarded Children." *Journal of Educational Psychology*, 69, 1977, 121–28.

Bartel, Nettie and Guskin, Samuel. "A Handicap as a Social Phenomenon" in *Psychology of Exceptional Children and Youth*, William M. Cruickshank (ed.). Englewood Cliffs, N.J. Prentice-Hall, 1980.

Cummings, R. W., & Cleborne, D. M. *Parenting the Learning Disabled: A Realistic Approach*. Springfield, IL, Charles C Thomas, 1985.

Dreikers, Rudolf. *Children: The Challenge*. New York: E. P. Dutton, 1987.

Flynn, George and Kowalczyk-McPhee, Bernie. "A School System in Transition." (unpublished manuscript) (no date)

Gerard, H. B., & Miller, N. *School Desegregation: A Long Range Study*. New York, Plenum, 1975.

Gersten, R., Walker, H., & Darch, C.: "Relationship Between Teachers' Effectiveness and Their Tolerance for Handicapped Students." *Exceptional Children*, 54(5), 1988, 433–438.

Glasser, William. *Control Theory In the Classroom*. New York, Harper and Row, 1986.

Haynes, M., & Jenkins, R. "Reading Instruction in Special Education Resource Rooms." *American Educational Research Journal*, 23(2), 1986, 161–190.

Janke, R. "The Teams-Games-Tournament (TGT) Method and the Behavioral Adjustment and Academic Achievement of Emotionally Impaired Adolescents." Paper presented at annual convention of American Educational Research Association, Toronto, 1978.

Johnson, David. *Circles of Learning*. Edina, MN, Interaction Book Company, 1984.

Kaufman, Gershen. *Shame, The Power of Caring*. Rochester, VT, Schenkan Books, Inc., 1985.

Keirsey, David and Bates, Marilyn. *Please Understand Me*. Del Mar, CA, Prometheus Nemesis Book Company, 1984.

Kelly, R.: Computers and sensory impaired individuals. In J. D. Lindsey (Ed.), *Computers and Exceptional Individuals*. Columbus, OH, Merrill, 1985.

Lerner, J.: *Learning Disabilities: Theories, Diagnosis, and Teaching Strategies*. Boston, Houghton Mifflin, 1989.

Lieberman, Lawrence. *Special Educator's Guide ... to regular education*. Newtonville, MA, GloWorm Publications, 1986.

Madden, N. A., & Slavin, R. E. "Cooperative Learning and Social Acceptance of Mainstreamed Academically Handicapped Students." *Journal of Special Education*, 17, 1983, 171–82.

Mercer, C.D., & Mercer, A. R.: *Teaching Students With Learning Problems.* Columbus, OH, Merrill, 1985.

National Commission on Excellence in Education, *A Nation at Risk.* A Report to the Nation and the Secretary of Education, United States Department of Education, 1983.

Nevin, A., Thousand, J., & Fox, W.: Promising practices: An inservice training model integrating severely handicapped learners. *Teacher Education and Special Education,* 10(1), 1987.

Newman, Judith M. (Ed.). *Whole Language.* Portsmouth, New Hampshire: Heinemann, 1985.

Peck, M. Scott. *The Different Drum.* New York, Simon and Schuster, 1987.

Reynolds, Maynard. "Past, Present, and Future of School Integration." In *Minnesota UAP Impact,* Volume 1 (2), Winter 1988. A report of the Minnesota University Affiliate Program on Developmental Disabilities. Minneapolis, MN, University of Minnesota.

Salvia, J., & Ysseldyke, J. *Assessment in Special and Remedial Education.* Boston, Houghton Mifflin, 1989.

Schaef, Anne Wilson. *Women's Reality.* Minneapolis, MN, Winston Press, 1981.

Slavin, R. E. "A Student Team Approach To Teaching Adolescents with Special Emotional and Behavioral Needs." *Psychology in the Schools,* 14 (1), 1977, 77–84.

Slavin, R. "Ability Grouping and Student Achievement in Elementary Schools; A Best Evidence Synthesis." *Review of Educational Research,* 57, 1987, 293–336.

Slavin, R. E., Madden, N. E., & Leavy, M. B. "Effects of Team Assisted Individualization on the Mathematics Achievement of Academically Handicapped and Nonhandicapped Students." *Journal of Educational Psychology,* 76, 1984, 813–19.

Smith, Frank. *Insult To Intelligence.* Portsmouth, NH, Heinemann, 1986.

"Overselling Literacy," *Phi Delta Kappan,* Vol. 70, January 1989.

Sprick, Randall. *Discipline in the Secondary Classroom.* Center for Applied Research in Education, NJ, 1985.

Sternberg, L., Taylor, R., & Schilt, J. *So You're Not A Special Educator.* Springfield, IL, Charles C Thomas, 1986.

Stiggins, R., Rubel, E., & Edys, Q.: *Measuring Thinking Skills in the Classroom.* Washington, D.C., National Education Association, 1988.

Tuttle, F., Becker, L., & Sousa, J.: *Program Design and Development for Gifted and Talented Students.* Washington, D.C., National Education Association, 1988.

Wang, M.C. & Walberg, H. J. (Eds.). *Adapting Instruction To Individual Differences.* Berkeley, CA: McCutchan, 1985.

Wang, M. C. & Birch, J. W. (Eds.). *Handbook of Special Education Research and Practice,* Vol. 1. London: Pergamon Press, 1987.

We would like to thank Mary Ann Rotondi, Amy Vargo, Ann Weis, and Mike Howard for their contributions.

7

USING COMPUTERS TO
STIMULATE INTERACTION, THINKING
AND COLLABORATION

It's language that makes us human,
Literacy that makes us civilized,
Technology that makes us powerful
And it's being in community with
others that makes us free.

A major difference between collaborative learning before the computer and today's situation is that now we have a technological tool that can allow for the dynamic exploration through time, space and ideas in an interactive way that was previously impossible. The computer can also provide connections to distant colleagues and even serve as a nonhuman collaborator. It may not be a reality today, but computers *will* become an integral part of the teaching and learning process. Once this happens, critical thinking may well take center stage as computers supplement regular textbook programs allowing students access to multiple sources of information and the ability to deal with questions that have many answers.

Computers are proliferating in classrooms around the country. In 1983 the U.S. Office of Education's estimate was 250,000 computers in the schools. Today, the number is approaching three million—and nearly all of the schools have at least one of them. The real question is whether computers are being used to amplify instruction in new ways. There is a difference in numbers and how computers are used in schools for poor children and schools for the more economically advantaged. And females across the board have less computer involvement than male students. In less affluent schools, district computers tend to be used for drill and practice. In wealthy districts, they are more frequently used for enrichment and teaching higher level thinking skills.[1]

---

1. Cole, M., Griffin, P., & Laboratory of Comparative Human Cognition: *Contextual Factors in Education: Improving Science and Mathematics Education for Minorities and Women.* Prepared for the Committee on Research in Mathematics, Science and Technology Education, National Research Council. Madison, WI, 1987.

There is a potential educational link between attending to the growing numbers of poor children, minority children, and immigrant children. Yet, schools have hardly responded to the curriculum changes implied by the computer revolution. Curricula, teaching habits, textbooks, and tests are all products of the precomputer age. And when computers are around they are usually not well integrated into classroom instruction. The change brought by computers *is* perceptible, but the potential of the technology will not be fully realized without systematic support and teacher training. Infatuation with technology is one thing, improving learning quite another.

Many argue that computers will not be used effectively in elementary and secondary classrooms until they are used in the learning experiences of teachers themselves. Therefore, there is increasing pressure to hire teachers who can use the technology effectively. The National Education Association recently called on every school district to provide computers for every teacher by the year 1991. But purchasing equipment, although a good start, will not automatically guarantee change.

To teach today's students effectively, it may be necessary to rethink content, classroom organization, methods of instruction, and the curriculum itself. This means moving beyond how to apply a new piece of computer software to redefining classroom experiences to fit the possibilities of today. This chapter will focus is on using computers for interactive collaboration —connecting peers, the curriculum, and new representations of knowledge. When computers are used imaginatively they allow students to follow their own interests and direct their own thinking and learning. Research on this aspect of educational computing and collaboration is more than sufficient to justify the use of both to accelerate student thinking and learning.[2]

Collaborative Learning with Computer Technology

The first computers in schools were seen as a flashy new way to provide more basic skill practice using surrogate "teacher talk." Lessons were programmed; students took their places in front of the screen and pushed buttons on the keyboard. No talking was needed once directions were given. The computer "taught"; the student was supposed to work

2. Vedder, P.H.: *Cooperative Learning: A Study on Processes and Effects of Cooperation Between Primary School Children.* The Hague, Stichting Voor Onderzoek van net Onderwijs, 1985.

Figure 15.

and listen in quiet isolation. But that part really didn't work out as planned. More frequently than not, students clustered together, sought advice from peer experts, and showed off their skill or product. Contrary to early fears, the use of computers tends to increase rather than decrease social skills. Unlike written sheets of paper, writing or graphics on a computer screen is looked upon as something public, more like a book or TV program.

The computer is a natural learning vehicle for cooperative group work. The educational computing skill practice model still exists, but increasingly programs are being enriched by interactivity. Software that builds on the uniqueness of the computer is making its way into classrooms or computer labs. The computer can now be used to collaboratively learn *how* to do a task—or as a tool for actually *doing* it. For example, students can use the computer to learn some elements of music (and math)—and use it to *make* music.

It took Johannes Kepler four years to calculate the orbit of Mars—today students can do in about four seconds using a microcomputer. Current information technologies have changed how we think and communicate. They have also vastly increased the capacity to know and do things in a more personalized way. There are new Apple II programs like *Critical Thinking and The One Computer Classroom* that are designed to help the classroom teacher build thinking skills across the curriculum.[3]

For those classrooms with Apple IIGS computers, MECC's *World Geo Graph* offers a powerful and easy-to-use data base that really changes the way students can interact with maps and each other.

Among the many untapped facets of computer use is the machine's ability to accommodate a wide range of learning styles. While reading directions on the computer screen appeals to a minority of students who operate well with print and listening learning styles, the computer also offers a rich array of graphics for those students who are more visual learners. Computers can be harnessed as tools for multiple ways of thinking. Like the pencil, ruler or compass, the computer's power lies in the user's thoughtful use. It's not the knowledge the computer can teach as much as it is the way students can use them to explore, compose, create, and experiment.

Computers are rapidly becoming part of elementary and secondary education throughout the country. Many schools have five or more computers.[4] A nationwide survey the Center for Social Organization of Schools estimated schools would need one computer for twelve students just to provide 30 minutes of computer time a day to all students. The current ratio is about 40 to 1. The extent to which computers are actually used varies. Surveys in 1987 found that while 70 percent of elementary teachers had access to computers, only 40 percent frequently used them.[5] Computers are now being used to teach and practice academic subject matter which was formerly presented through lecture or printed materials. Simulation, critical thinking and problem-solving software is used more

---

3. Tom Synder Productions, 90 Sherman St., Cambridge, MA 02140.

4. Becker, H. J. Our National Report Card: Preliminary Results from the New Johns Hopkins Survey. *Classroom Computer Learning*, 6(4), 30–3, 1986.

5. Ponte et al., Evaluation of an Instructional Computing Inservice Course for Elementary and Middle School Teachers. *School Science and Mathematics*, 86(5), 375–385, 1986.

infrequently.[6] Simulation software, for example, provides more than electronic textbooks. Students can replicate science experiments, re-create historical events or model business activities. Variables can be altered, the program can be stopped at any stage and parts of experiments can be reexamined or repeated. New programs, like *Geometric Supposer,* have no predetermined instructional agendas and allow students to collaboratively explore through direct observation, measurement, and experimentation.[7]

Word processing programs, data base and spreadsheet systems have also found practical applications in schools. Some data base programs come with templates for specific subjects, such as social studies, spreadsheets are used in teaching mathematics, and graphing programs are used in algebra and geometry, and programs like TK! Solver, Think Tank and Idea Processor are finding their way into school use. And various versions of Logo have proven that it can foster social interaction and foster the principles of cooperative learning.[8]

Computers in the Classroom

In the last five years we began to see educational software which used the computer's unique characteristics to enhance the learning process. Language arts and English teachers began to incorporate word processing applications, spelling and style checkers giving students powerful new tools for interacting with their writing. In the natural and social sciences, simulations have provided students with innovative experiments and surrogate experiences from history. Information can be embedded in visual narratives to create context that gives meaning to dry facts. Applications in biology, chemistry, engineering, ergonomics, physics, psychology and physiology allow teachers to create simulations which conform to the normal laws of the universe.

The research suggests that students benefit when they are given control over system parameters so they can explore their effects.[9] New

6. Kloosterman, P., Ault, P., & Harty, H. School-Based Computer Education: Practices and Trends. *Educational Technology,* 25(5), 35–38, 1985.

7. Yerushalmy, M., Chazan, D., & Gorden, M. *Guided Inquiry and Technology: A Year Long Study of Children and Teachers Using the Geometric Supposer.* Technical Report 88-6, Cambridge, MA, Educational Technology Center, Harvard University Graduate School of Education, 1987.

8. Maddux, C.D., & Johnson, D.L. *Logo: Methods and Curriculum for Teachers.* New York, Haworth Press, 1988.

9. Center for Social Organization of Schools. *Instructional Uses of School Computers: Reports from the 1985 National Survey.* Baltimore, MD, The Johns Hopkins University, June 1986.

computer software, such as *Gravity of the Planets*, allows students to discover algebraic rules making reasonable estimates about weight and forces of gravity. Students concoct their own problems, such as the weight of the class, pooling resources and information. Working in groups, students discuss, plan and experiment together. In a similar cooperative vein students can explore museums or works of art—calling up visuals and printed text to explain the history and elaborate the conditions under which the work was created. Thinking skills can be developed differently in the fine arts. The experience of art, for example, cannot be reduced to empirically tested concepts like those that dominate science.[10] Through the collaborative use of computers, art can emerge as an even more important source of spiritual information.

Computers have been found to increase socialization among students. The curriculum materials that are most effective and most popular are those that provide for social interaction.[11] Students can collaborate by working in pairs on even the more traditional programs. And capitalizing on computer-controlled interactive activities can reach small groups of children through many senses.

New Student and Teacher Roles

Collective genius is nothing more than knowing
how to arrange for the right use of tools.
—Samual Johnson

The successful use of computers means involving students and educators in the learning process in new ways. As with any medium, the vitality of computer use depends on talented teachers. Professional knowledge about children, learning, curricula and classroom organization goes hand in hand with the competencies needed to apply courseware sensibly. Helped along with informed adult energy, computers can do more than facilitate the exchange of ideas and improve writing skills.[12] They can help sharpen a student's power to think critically and develop independent judgments.

---

10. Gardner, H. Perkins, D. (Eds.). *Art, Mind, and Education: Research from Project Zero.* Ithaca, NY, University of Illinois Press, 1989.

11. Mandell, C.J., and Mandell, S.L.: *Computers in Education Today.* St. Paul, MN, West Publishing Co., 1989.

12. The Office of Technology Assessment: *Power On! New Tools for Teaching and Learning.* Washington, D.C., U.S. Government Printing Office, 1988.

The teacher has many roles in structuring collaboration on computers. They include:

- assigning students to mixed-ability teams
- establishing positive interdependence
- teaching cooperative social skills
- ensuring individual accountability
- helping groups process information

The purpose of team assignment is to ensure a heterogeneous mix of students taking into account ability levels, language differences, race, culture, sex and behavior patterns. If students haven't worked together before, some structured team-building activities will result in fewer problems later on. These may include designing such things as a personal team profile, a group poster or slogan using the computer. It is important to establish good starting points rather than having to backtrack later on to solve problems.

Collaboration with computers is not restricted to pairs of students. Teams are frequently formed by pooling resources between several computer pairs—or combining an assignment after each partnership has completed their work. Students provide each other with additional information or the specific technical information needed to carry out tasks. Peer tutoring can flourish in such a team-centered computer environment.

Establishing feelings of positive interdependence is another role of the teacher. Students should understand why it's important for them to work together and what is to be learned in the process. Promoting feelings that *no one is successful unless everyone is successful* shapes the way students interact with each other. If this objective is not communicated, students may revert back to traditional individualistic roles out of habit. Methods for getting this point across to students include structuring:

- *Goal Interdependence* —stating clearly what each member of the group should know how to do upon completion of the task
- *Task interdependence* —clearly defining the group goal and what the team should agree on or be able to produce
- *Resource Interdependence* —specifying parameters, materials, the team's task
- *Role Interdependence* —reviewing the individual roles for the group members; keyboarder, checker, reporter, summarizer, encourager, etc. Set up the expectation that everyone is responsible for explaining how they came up with the answer. Explain the grading procedures,

group credit as well as credit for how well each student performs their group job.

Teachers are also involved in teaching of social skills and monitoring to make sure that students continue to use the skill. Teachers select the skill roles they want to teach and emphasize the cooperative strategies to be exhibited by all members. Ensuring individual accountability involves making sure that each group member participated; that no student dominated the computer activity or hitchhiked on the group's work without giving their share.

By structuring individual accountability the teacher guarantees ongoing group participation and satisfaction with the group's learning activities. Successful teachers employ a mix of activities like: individual interviews, work samples, random member questioning, collecting individual papers at random, or asking individuals to explain the group product. In addition to observing and assisting groups, the teacher is also responsible for processing what was learned in the group activity and making sure that teams reflect on what they did and evaluate the team's efforts.

Challenging work on the computer is particularly effective in collaborative work. Activities which involve decision making, data display choices, varying scales and complicated data manipulations lend themselves to cooperative group work. Many activities involve work on and off the computer. Decisions about the division of labor, topic exploration, presentation format are off computer activities. Library searches, surveys, and data collection are also activities that often precede computer use. Finding information, manipulating variables, thinking critically, composing as a group, adjusting, arranging, sorting out what is important, and collaboratively producing a product are all habits that will help students participate in the knowledge work force of the twenty-first century.

Sharing responsibility entails dividing the work, typing, proofreading, analyzing graphs and text, providing direction, and critically analyzing the decisions made. Students can work on the computer in pairs, sharing roles and making sure that they and their teammates make the best use of the equipment and understand what's happening.

Even the most successful use of computers in the classroom will not solve our serious social and educational problems. But failing to use the medium will leave the schools less able to cope with these difficulties. Becoming competent and confident users of this technology is important if the schools are to meet the demands of a changing society. It is equally important to understand the social, economic, political and educational contexts of the technology that shapes our lives. As these "smart machines" enter into grand alliances with other technologies, they will become common adjuncts to the human teacher and peer group.

There is a social context in which students and teachers interact with computers. In the world outside of school, computers are seen as real collaborative tools for real people. A similar view would be appropriate for schools. Teachers may have to make some changes in how they teach, but computers can never serve as electronic teacher replacements. There is no substitute for educational leaders who bring an "informed exuberance" to the learning environment.

Computers are not for dispensing isolated learning, like the teaching machines of yesteryear. They are instruments to meet integrated social and curricular goals. Computer programs can facilitate thought while serving as a unique and useful supplement to paper, pencils and books. They can also be used for peer tutoring, peer criticism, and group work. Working on computers in cooperative pairs is usually better for beginners than working alone. Sharing with peers, in a supportive small group, is just as important when learning with computers as it is with any other medium.

Computers are only a part of a much broader technological revolution. In the early days instructional television programs and computer software were passive. This is changing. Just as news programming and videodiscs have enlivened video, the best new computer programs make computing interactive. Peer sharing and coaching can add more active elements to a computer program that is not all that engaging. In opening up avenues of communication, educators must decide which technology is best for which students and which set of objectives fit the technology. By the time students get to high school they should be able to develop genuine group goals and use computers to access information, process words, create images and solve problems.

Two undisputed directions for schools to consider in the future is making greater use of appropriate technologies and collaboration. . . . Multiple ongoing revolutions in technology and classroom organization will require schools to prepare students to make wise choices in the face of an overabundance of information.

—Michael Marien

SELECTING AND EVALUATING SOFTWARE

The current climate of educational reform has created an opportunity for teachers to become leaders of the effort to create schools that are better places to teach and learn in a spirit of cooperation. As they are called upon to become more sophisticated managers of students' learning, teachers increasingly use computers to help students think through their decisions, allowing them to see the potential consequences of different actions.

Using computers, like using any other media, should be directed at achieving some instructional purpose. This goes beyond having a few computer programs in a learning center at the back of the room where a student goes when everything else is done. Computers can be used to teach traditional content and open doors to knowledge in ways that other media can't.

Competency needs vary according to the discipline being taught, the curriculum, and the grade level. Most teachers would not think of assigning a chapter from the history or science book without some kind of lead in and some follow-up activity. The same thing is true for learning on computers. Students should not be left to fend for themselves when the computer enters the process. Like any good learning material, computer software needs to be enhanced and extended by an enthusiastic instructor.

Choosing computer courseware is heavily influenced by content and lesson objectives as well as the abilities and skills of the student groups involved. As teachers look for software that is adaptive to cooperative learning situations, it may be helpful to ask several questions:

1. What skill is the program trying to teach? And is this a skill that fits into my curricular objectives for cooperative learning?
2. Does the computer courseware create high levels of engagement for student groups?
3. What examples does the program use to teach these skills?
4. What kinds of teaching techniques are used in the program?
5. What prerequisite skills do students need to use this piece of software?
6. Where does this piece of software fit into the learning sequence for this topic?
7. What directions or precomputer activities need to be provided to student teams before using the software?

8. What group activities could serve as a follow up to this software program?
9. How will individual accountability and group performance be evaluated?
10. What other materials would enhance the skills developed by this program?

There are time-consuming evaluation issues surrounding the multitude of software programs to be dealt with. Simulation, Logo microworlds, word processing, interactive literature, spreadsheets, data base managers, expert (AI) systems or getting the computer in contact with the outside world (telecommunications) through a modem/software combination all increase the potential for influencing impressionable minds. That is too large a universe for the teacher to figure out alone. Other teachers who use computers are an excellent source of help with what works in the classroom. Students can also take some of the responsibility. This task is more reasonable and the analysis process itself is an excellent learning vehicle.

It's important to consider whether or not a particular piece of software is motivating and easy to integrate into their instructional program. But the bottom line is: *Do the students like it?* Without question, teachers and students are the ones who experience the consequences of making good or bad choices in software selection. And they are the ones who most quickly learn the consequences of poor choices.

Criteria for Cooperative Learning Software Evaluation

Any software program can be adapted for use in a cooperative learning lesson. To get maximum results from the computer as well as to benefit from the range of skills of the cooperative group the following criteria may be helpful:

1. Does the software empower the group making them more productive than they would be without using the program?
2. Is the software adaptable? Can the team add their own problems or alter the sequence of the program?
3. Does the software meet the age, attention span and interests of your student groups?
4. Does the program develop, supplement or enhance the curricular skills you're trying to teach?

5. Is the software easy to use for both teacher and student groups? Does the program require adult supervision or instruction?
6. Groups need to actively control what the program does. To what extent does the program allow this?
7. Can the courseware be modified to meet group learning needs and adjusted to the varied learning styles of the members?
8. Does the program have animated graphics which enliven the lesson?
9. Does the program meet instructional objectives and is it educationally sound?
10. Does the program involve higher level thinking and problem solving?

Adapting Software for Collaboration:
A Few New Favorites

Adventures With Charts and Graphs: Project Zoo
National Geographic

Checkerboard Trails
Focus Media

Fraction Concepts
MECC

Fantavision IIGS
Broderbund

Kemeny/Kurtz Math Series
True Basic Inc.

MusicPrinter Plus
Temporal Acuity Products

How the West Was Won + Three × Four

National Inspirer
Tom Synder Publications

Word Bench
Addison-Wesley

Calendar Crafter
MECC

Explore-A-Story: The Best Bubble Blower and Explore-A-Science: Animal Watch
DC Heath

Deluxe Paint II
Electronic Arts

816 Paint
Baudville

Pathfinder
Sunburst

Easy Street
Mindplay

Go Fish
Queue Inc.

Playing With Science: Temperature
Sunburst

Sailing Through Story Problems
Developmental Learning Materials

Activities and Strategies for the
Cooperative Learning Computer Classroom

Group Software activities:

After a group has completed a software assignment, have the team try one of these activities.

- Make up a quiz about the program and give the questions to another group in the class who has used the program.
- Create your own soundtrack for part of the program.
- Make up a student guide for the program. Use your own directions and illustrations.
- Interview other students who have used the program and write down their responses.
- Write a group review of the program for a magazine.

Integration with Other Materials

After having students use a program involving a subject or theme, assign student teams to research the topic by finding books, films or TV programs around the same issue. Encourage comparisons between both sets of materials. Have students use the simulation program again and offer insights into the lesson based on their findings. If you have the documentation (instructions) that goes along with the program, then you have another whole set of activities.

Skills Practice Tournament

This activity is designed to be used with drill and practice software which reinforces concepts taught but not mastered by students. (Practice on multiplication facts, spelling words, etc., fall into this category.) If students are unfamiliar with the software program, demonstrate the program they will be using. Allow time to answer questions, provide practice demonstrations, etc. Once students are familiar with program:

1. Divide the class into learning teams to practice desired concepts. Structure the teams so that students of varying ability levels are on all teams. Instruct students to practice with their team using the drill and practice software program. Allow time for each team to polish their skills and master the concepts.

2. When students feel their teams are ready, split up the teams into two- to three-person tournament tables composed of members of differ-

ent teams. It's a good idea to select tournament teams whose members are of similar ability levels (for example, students who have performed well on this skill would be grouped together on one tournament table, and students who were having more difficulty would be grouped together on another.)

3.   Using the same piece of software, team representatives try to win points for their team. Each student from a tournament table might play 3 or 4 rounds of a drill and practice activity and keep a record of right and wrong answers for each member of the tournament table.

4.   After the tournament, the people at each table with the highest scores (greatest number of correct answers) receive 6 points to take back to their team. Those with the second highest scores receive 4 points, those with the least highest number receive 2 points. Winning teams are determined by total team scores.

Strategies for Team Learning

Before having teams start with the software it is important to plan the lesson, state objectives, select supporting materials, manipulatives, etc. and set students up for success. Many software programs lend themselves to precomputer lessons, whether solving problems with manipulative materials such as attribute blocks, creating group compositions, graphics or doing spreadsheet applications. It is helpful for the group to have encountered the concept before beginning the software or computer lesson. It is also useful to demo the program for the group using a computer overhead projector, stopping to ask questions, give directions and receive input. This saves teaching time later on.

Many teachers are facing the problem of having only one computer in the class. By setting up activities for both on and off the computer groups, rotate materials and computer time. By demonstrating and answering questions with the whole class, additional efficiency is gained when the group encounters the computer task.

Collaborative Writing with Computers

Writing in collaborative groups is an important instructional use of the computer. Through such collaboration students learn strategies for negotiation and conflict resolution. The isolation of the individual writer is relieved by working with a writing group which shares a common task.

Motivation is easier to sustain when student writers feel responsible not only to a teacher but to each other. Most important, collaborative writing groups offer students a real audience—which is built in to every step of the writing process (Bruffee, 1983). Students give and receive immediate feedback with each other, and as the group becomes more familiar with each member's strengths and idiosyncrasies, a method for effective group work evolves.

With the addition of new computer lines like Apple Macintosh, the power and facility of writing is greatly enhanced at every level. Word processing is as easy as finding the correct keys on the keyboard. Using software like MacWrite, MicrosoftWord, MacDraw, MacPaint, and CricketGraph programs, group writing takes on a professional look. Teams can choose from a variety of strategies which emphasize and build on the members' particular strengths. Here are some possible models:

Whole Team Approach

1. The team plans and outlines the writing project. The sections are divided among the group. Each member drafts a part. The team meets to compile the parts and revises the whole.

2. Another alternative to the team approach:

Team plans and outlines. One member writes entire draft. Team revises.

3. In the third model the team plans and writes the draft together. Half of the team revises the draft without consulting the other team members. The group meets to discuss revisions and make final decisions.

One-Member Emphasis

In this model one team member plans and writes draft. The team revises.

Assignment Emphasis

One member assigns writing tasks. Each member carries out individual tasks. One member compiles the parts and revises the whole. Another model with students working in pairs one member dictates. Another person transcribes and revises.[13]

An individual writer's satisfaction with the collaborative writing task is often influenced by several factors:

---

13. Gaard, G.: *Collaborative Theory and Collaborative Practice In the Electronic Classroom.* University of Minnesota, Paper presented 1989 MCTE conference, 1989.

Control	• the degree of control the writer has over the text
Credit	• the way credit is given
Response	• the ability to respond to others who may modify the text
Procedure	• an agreed-upon procedure for solving disputes among coauthors
Flexibility	• the amount of flexibility tolerated in using pre-established formats
Constraints	• the number and kind of constraints imposed on the writers (deadlines, length and style requirements)
Status	• the status of the project within the group

Working as a group challenges the group to combine the various skills of its members to find new connections for getting the job done faster and easier than would have been possible alone. Certainly, difference can be viewed as a drawback, if difference is not stressed as an asset and students are not encouraged to talk about each writer's idiosyncrasies so these can be utilized in their collaborative strategy.

Student writers will tend to view their group activity as more important if it is given adequate time in class.[14] Though many elementary schools are working towards preparing students for computer use, at this stage many high school and college teachers are still introducing first-time users to computers. By providing instructional and peer support for students learning to use computers, writing programs perform a valuable function in preparing students for the writing and group work skills so necessary in today's world.

COMPUTERS AND THINKING SKILLS

The capacity for technological change often precedes our understanding of the impact that change will have. When it comes to collaboratively using computers to build thinking skills and knowledge of different disciplines, change is visible before its implications are comprehended. Basic skills, computing, critical and creative thinking need each other. Spontaneity and the creative imagination are elements of achievement that are central to the development of human thinking and freedom. There is no creative thinking or freedom in a solitary vacuum. A person

---

14. Allen, N., Atkinson, D., Morgan, M., Moore, T., & Snow, C. What experienced collaborators say about collaborative writing. *Journal of Business and Technical Communication*, 1, 1987.

with a creative style of thinking needs to be stimulated by others. Creative abilities, like connecting disparate concepts or giving novel ideas a chance, requires a mix of traits and abilities. And, when teaching thinking is the question, it is always time to begin. Computer-based learning technologies can embody powerful ideas which can be shared across subject areas.

The Interaction Between Creative Thinking and Basic Skills

The intellectual tools developed in one area can foster originality and critical thinking in another. Skills can combine with creative factors to generate learning across a wide range of subjects. Skill without imagination is sterile, while imagination without disciplined skill aborts its image. Although basic and imaginative skills may seem antithetical, one without the other is limiting. In reading, you need a few basic subskills to get started—but without the higher level context of good literature and imaginative thinking it leads nowhere. The reverse situation is equally dismal—a great imagination can destroy its potential without at least some skills being in place.

No matter how creative a concept, there is an implicit connection to subskills. For either basic or thinking skills to be developed requires that each area support the other. It is fine to challenge the framework of narrowness often associated with "the basics," for without connections to higher levels of thinking they lead nowhere. The two areas have a curiously symbiotic relationship. A major difficulty which most teachers encounter is getting students to depart from the skills framework in a disciplined and informed fashion. Computer-based technology can be an informed associate in this process.

There is little question that educational computing has a role to play in helping students develop an unconditional positive regard for one another. Computing would seem to be a natural bridge between the old view of "the basics," thinking skills, and breaking through the artificial limits of school-imposed social isolation. Good teachers can make this technology one more tool in the effort to inspire students to approach their education with a sense of responsibility and possibility.

The Computer as an Expressive Medium and Skill Builder

Computers are not good or bad: they are powerful. Like words, paint, or clay, the computer can also be used as an expressive medium. Skills and imagination belong together. In mathematics, for example, the act of creating requires a prerequisite skill base of mathematical structure and pattern. Poetry also relies on the writer's mastery of language, form and meter. The computer is a medium of human expression which can be used as an extension of these skills and creativity. Imagination and the basics, poetry and mathematics can emerge from the technology together.

The flexibility of computers allows the imagination to select and combine elements on various levels. Mathematical patterns found in nature, like fractiles, can be generated so that visual models are easily manipulated on the computer for creative problem solving. Thus, the computer allows students to learn problem solving and basic skills in a more dynamic manner.

Like composers who create by sitting at the piano and making things up, the computer also permits creative play. This aspect of computers deserves at least equal time with basic skill building. Children using a Logo program, for example, can manipulate complex geometric concepts in math while creating their own visual compositions with musical accompaniment. The editing process allows them to add, delete and "arrange" to their satisfaction.

Computer-generated visual models—whether basic skills or flights of fancy—can be manipulated with flexibility and creativity. The opportunity is created for moving across media using computer graphics, numbers, words or music. Children create their own microworlds, imagine, *and* build skills which can be freely explored. The computer provides a language of thinking and a means of expression where permission is granted to be oneself.

The traditional notion of educators is that if fluency, flexibility, and originality were systematically taught, true creativity would follow. Unfortunately, it isn't that simple. To begin with, teachers have to teach it. Secondly, fluency doesn't count for much if all the ideas generated are simply trivial. And if flexibility clouds issues or discourages group decision making it can impede learning. Even originality might be simply a social accommodation, rather than either intuitive boundary-pushing or barrier breaking. We need to question some of our most basic assumptions about fostering basic skill.

Unfortunately, the most common school practice encourages children to be plodders who see the rules as conduits for action, rather than as collaborative springboards for changing realities. Taking risks, dealing with failure, the desire to be surprised, and enjoying ambiguity are all essential elements in creative behavior. All are difficult for teachers to model and for many students to accept. After all, simply accepting the directions from someone in authority is always easier.

In the real world we learn more about creativity from our failures, accidents, and the personal restructuring of our reality in the face of uncertainty. Gaining the help of a supportive group reduces the fear of failure. This fear prevents some students from even trying creative activities. The computer can rekindle interest by allowing the students to take risks and make mistakes without a loss of self-esteem.

As a dynamic communication instrument the computer can act as a generator for collaboration, creativity, and skill-building. Students, even if they are great distances apart, can use the computer and a modem to jointly create new ideas and look at basic skills in a new way. Computers can also give visual dimension to metaphors and help students go beyond the literal in understanding what they are reading and writing about. What better way is there to ensure that the basics are taught in depth, than to include the basic intellectual tools and symbol systems—reinforced through exploratory computer-based instruction?

The Future of Human-Machine Interaction

The 1990's will bring increasingly powerful multimedia computers into the educational system. Even today it's possible to connect to a video-disc and CD ROM player. The synthesis of visual, auditory and manual cues goes along with the new emphasis on empowering students and teachers. We already have more technology and software than we know how to use. Once we get a handle on them, technological tools can help creativity and inventiveness permeate all aspects of a child's learning. This process requires fresh metaphors and fresh pedagogical ideas to manage the computerization that is transforming our educational environment.

As tomorrow's schools struggle with social change, new technology, a rapidly expanding knowledge base and a multicultural school population, there is an ever-increasing need to help students understand basic skills *and* develop higher order thinking abilities. As we all work to manage our own learning—both present and future—the ability to creatively

Communication technologies

Figure 16.

think and solve problems cooperatively will become more important than ever. Working creatively with conflicts means viewing them as possibilities for the cooperative improvement of computer-based education.

As schools move through the next decade computers will be viewed as just one part of the technology equation. The school microcomputers of the early eighties were the electronic learning equivalent of the worksheet. Computers are now multimedia devices capable of full motion video, voice recognition, interactive graphics and touch-sensitive screens. With the right software and peripheral devices, PCs can now turn a disk of data into a book in a few minutes, making high-quality personalized publishing a reality. And Steve Jobs wants nothing less than "the *world* in a backpack." His NeXT computer already has a large *island* or two on CD–ROM. The world will prove more difficult. Technology and educational development decisions made today will be with us at the beginning of the new millennium. Experts predict that in the twenty-first century we will have self-improving thinking machines that seem more like living things.[15]

The computer monitor is beginning to bring us more than print and

15. Moravec, H.: *Mind Children: The Future of Robot and Human Intelligence*. Cambridge, MA, Harvard University Press, 1988.

simple graphics. Multimedia or hypermedia information combines moving video, sound, animation, and printed words. New programs, like Apple's *HyperCard*, allow information to be set up in a way that allows different learning styles to be accommodated. Using these programs, learners can selectively hop down a variety of learning alleys. As users communicate and weave knowledge in their personal way they will need new, more flexible thinking skills to surf through the waves of information.

REFERENCES

Adams, D., & Hamm, M.: *Electronic Learning.* Springfield, IL, Charles C Thomas, 1987.

Adams, D., & Hamm, M.: *Educational Computing: Issues, Trends and a Practical Guide.* Springfield, IL, Charles C Thomas, 1986.

Allen, N., Atkinson, D., Morgan, M., Moore, T., & Snow, C.: What experienced collaborators say about collaborative writing. *Journal of Business and Technical Communication,* 1, 70–90, 1987.

Becker, H. J. Our National Report Card: Preliminary Results from the New Johns Hopkins Survey. *Classroom Computer Learning,* 6(4), 30–3, 1986.

Bruffee, K. A.: Writing and Reading as Collaborative or Social Acts. In J.N. Hays, J.R. Ramsey, & R.D. Foulke (Eds.), *The Writer's Mind: Writing as a Mode of Thinking.* (pp. 159–169). NCTE, 1983.

Center for Social Organization of Schools. *Instructional Uses of School Computers: Reports from the 1985 National Survey.* Baltimore, MD, The Johns Hopkins University, June 1986.

Cole, M., Griffin, P., & Laboratory of Comparative Human Cognition: *Contextual Factors in Education: Improving Science and Mathematics Education for Minorities and Women.* Prepared for the Committee on Research in Mathematics, Science and Technology Education, National Research Council. Madison, WI, 1987.

Costanzo, W.: *The Electronic Text: Learning to Write, Read, and Reason with Computers.* Englewood Cliffs, NJ, Educational Technology Publications, 1989.

Ede, L., & Lunsford, A.: Why Write ... Together: A Research Update. *Rhetoric Review,* 5(1), 71–81, 1986.

Erikson, T.: *Off and Running: The Computer Off-line Activities Book.* Berkeley, CA, EQUALS, 1986.

Felici, J., & Nace, T.: *Desktop Publishing Skills.* Reading, MA: Addison-Wesley, 1987.

Franklin, S.: *Making the Literature, Writing, Word Processing Connection: The Best of the Writing Notebook 1983-1987.* Mendocino, CA: The Writing Notebook, 1987.

Gaard, G.: Collaborative Theory and Collaborative Practice In the Electronic Classroom. University of Minnesota. Paper presented at 1989 MCTE Conference, 1989.

Gardner, H.: *Art, Mind and Brain: A Cognitive Approach To Creativity.* New York: Basic Books, 1982.

Goldenberg, E. P., & Wallace, F.: *Exploring Language with Logo.* Cambridge, MA, MIT Press, 1987.

Hofstadter, D.: *Metamagical Themes: Questing for the Essence of Mind and Pattern.* New York: Basic Books, 1985.

ICCE: *Appleworks for Educators: A Beginner's Workbook.* Eugene, ICCE, University of Oregon, 1787 Agate St., Eugene, OR 97403.

Kloosterman, P., Ault, P., & Harty, H. School-Based Computer Education: Practices and Trends. *Educational Technology,* 25(5), 35–38, 1985.

Maddux, C.D., & Johnson, D.L.: *Logo: Methods and Curriculum for Teachers.* New York, Haworth Press, 1988.

Mandell, C.J., and Mandell, S.L.: *Computers in Education Today.* St. Paul, MN, West Publishing Co., 1989.

Moravec, H.: *Mind Children: The Future of Robot and Human Intelligence.* Cambridge, MA, Harvard University Press, 1988.

The Office of Technology Assessment: *Power On! New Tools for Teaching and Learning.* Washington, D.C., U.S. Government Printing Office, 1988.

Pagnoni, M. *Computers and Small Fries.* Garden City Park, NY, Avery, 1987.

Pea, R., & Sheingold, K.: *Mirrors of Minds: Patterns of Experience in Educational Computing.* Norwood, NJ, Ablex, 1987.

Perkins, D. N., Lochhead, J., & Bishop, J.: *Transfer and Teaching Thinking.* Hillsdale, NJ, Lawrence Erlbaum Associates, 1987.

Ponte et al., Evaluation of an Instructional Computing Inservice Course for Elementary and Middle School Teachers. *School Science and Mathematics,* 86(5), 375–385, 1986.

Rheingold, H.: *Tools for Thought: The People and Ideas Behind the Next Computer Revolution.* New York, Simon & Schuster, 1985.

Roberts, N. et al. *Integrating Computers Into the Elementary and Middle School.* Old Tappan, NJ, Prentice-Hall, 1988.

Schulman, E., & Page, R. *Spreadsheets for Beginners.* New York, Franklin Watts, 1987.

Solomon, C. *Computer Environments for Children: A Reflection on Theories of Learning and Education.* Cambridge, MA, MIT Press, 1986.

Swigger, K. M., and Swigger, B. K. Social patterns and computer use among pre-school children. *AEDS Journal.* 17(3), 1984.

Thomas, R. *ClassWorks: Appleworks for the Classroom.* Eugene, ICCE, 1988.

U.S. Congress of Technology Assessment. *Power On! New Tools for Teaching and Learning.* Washington, D.C., U. S. Government Printing Office.

Vedder, P.H. *Cooperative Learning: A Study on Processes and Effects of Cooperation Between Primary School Children.* The Hague, Stichting Voor Onderzoek van net Onderwijs, 1985.

Webb, N.M. Cognitive requirements of learning computer programming in group and individual settings. *AEDS Journal,* 18(3), 1985.

Williams, K. *Technologies of Control: The New Interactive Media for the Home.* Madison, University of Wisconsin Press, 1988.

Yerushalmy, M., Chazan, D., & Gorden, M. *Guided Inquiry and Technology: A Year Long Study of Children and Teachers Using the Geometric Supposer.* Technical Report 88-6, Cambridge, MA, Educational Technology Center, Harvard University Graduate School of Education, 1987.

AUTHOR INDEX

SUBJECT INDEX